# SOUND CHANGE

MLBD SERIES IN LINGUISTICS

General Editor
DHANESH JAIN

Volume XIV

# SOUND CHANGE

D N S Bhat

MOTILAL BANARSIDASS PUBLISHERS
PRIVATE LIMITED • DELHI

*First Edition: Delhi, 2001*



ISBN: 81-208-1766-4

*Also available at:*
MOTILAL BANARSIDASS
236, 9th Main III Block, Jayanagar, Bangalore 560 011
41 U.A. Bungalow Road, Jawahar Nagar, Delhi 110 007
8 Mahalaxmi Chamber, Warden Road, Mumbai 400 026
120 Royapettah High Road, Mylapore, Chennai 600 004
Sanas Plaza, 1302 Baji Rao Road, Pune 411 002
8 Camac Street, Calcutta 700 017
Ashok Rajpath, Patna 800 004
Chowk, Varanasi 221 001

*Printed in India*
BY JAINENDRA PRAKASH JAIN AT SHRI JAINENDRA PRESS,
A-45 NARAINA, PHASE-I, NEW DELHI 110 028
AND PUBLISHED BY NARENDRA PRAKASH JAIN FOR
MOTILAL BANARSIDASS PUBLISHERS PRIVATE LIMITED,
BUNGALOW ROAD, DELHI 110 007

# CONTENTS

# PREFACE

This is the revised and enlarged version of the book first published in 1972. All the chapters have been redrafted. The second chapter of the first edition has been removed and the points relevant to the present edition have been shifted to other chapters, especially to the one on reconstruction. Additional illustrative examples have been added in most places. As a result, the chapter on reconstruction is four times its original size.

The first chapter lists and evaluates different kinds of evidence that form the basis for postulating sound changes. The second chapter examines the most important characteristics of sound change, namely regularity and irreversibility. It also shows how some of the additional characteristics that are generally ascribed to sound change are yet to be authenticated.

The third chapter describes various effects that sound changes can have upon the structuring of language. It examines them from five different points of view and shows how these provide different classifications of these effects. The last chapter examines the two well-known methods of reconstruction—internal and comparative—and shows how these could be due to several procedures of reconstruction. It also points out that the validity of each of these procedures depends upon the validity of the underlying hypothesis.

The first edition of the book was much appreciated by students and teachers. An effort has been made to make this revised version even more accessible to them by including suggestions for further reading at the end of each chapter, and by providing a set of exercises for each chapter at the end of the book. An appendix lists all the sound changes described in the book, which could form the basis for additional exercises.

Mysore — D N S BHAT

24 May 2000

# 1

# EVIDENCE FOR SOUND CHANGE

## 1.1 Introduction

The term "sound change" is used as a technical term in historical linguistics. It refers to a change in the *pronunciation* of sounds. It takes place at the time in which a given generation of speakers is acquiring its first language. As a change in the pronunciation of sounds, it can either be conditioned or unconditioned. However, only sounds can constrain its occurrence. Aspects of grammar, lexicon, meaning, function etc. do not have any influence upon its occurrence. It is in this sense that sound change has been described as highly regular or "mechanical" and as having no exceptions.

Consider, for example, the change of initial *k* to *c* and *g* to *j* that has taken place in a dialect of Kannada, spoken by some of the communities in Hosur, Mysore district. It is a conditioned sound change in the sense that it has taken place only when there was a palatal vowel (*i, i:, e* or *e:*) occurring after it. The two consonants, *k* and *g*, remained unchanged in other environments. Its conditioning factor is also purely phonetic. It has affected all the words in which the sounds *k* or *g* occurred before a palatal vowel (see 1a), but it has not affected any of the words in which the two sounds occurred in other phonetic environments (see 1b).

| (1a) | *Gloss* | *Standard Kannada* | *Hosur Kannada* |
|---|---|---|---|
| | ear | *kivi* | *civi* |
| | work | *kelasa* | *celsa* |
| | hear | *ke:ḷu* | *ce:ḷu* |
| | parrot | *giḷi* | *jiṇi* |
| | scratch | *gi:ru* | *ji:ru* |
| | branch | *gellu* | *jellu* |

| (1b) | | | |
|---|---|---|---|
| | hair | *ku:dalu* | *ku:dlu* |
| | intestine | *karaḷu* | *kaḷḷu* |
| | call | *kare* | *kari* |
| | wall | *go:ḍe* | *gva:ḍe* |
| | hut | *guḍisalu* | *guḍḷu* |

On the other hand, the change of *ṇ* to *n* that has taken place in the Sapaliga dialect of Tulu is an unconditioned sound change. It has affected all the words in which the sound *ṇ* occurred earlier irrespective of the environment in which it occurred.

| (2) | *Gloss* | *Shivalli* | *Sapaliga* |
|---|---|---|---|
| | pinch | *kiṇkɨ* | *kinkɨ* |
| | hear | *ke:ṇɨ* | *ke:nɨ* |
| | elder brother | *aṇṇɛ* | *annɛ* |
| | corpse | *puṇa* | *puna* |
| | nail | *a:ṇi* | *a:ni* |
| | tick | *uṇŋgu* | *nuŋgu* |
| | jar | *baraṇi* | *barni* |

In addition to sound change, there can be other types of change that also affect the sounds of a language. For example, there can be grammar-oriented changes, called "analogical changes", that alter or remove some of the morphophonemic alternations of sounds introduced by earlier sound changes. Similarly, there can be word-oriented changes, called "sporadic" changes, which alter the phonetic structure or phonetic content of words individually. There can also be borrowing of words from neighbouring languages or dialects that introduce new sounds into a language.

An example for grammar-oriented change can be given from Kannada. There was a morphophonemic alternation in Old Kannada between *e*, *o* and *i*, *u* respectively, occurring in the case of a set of verbal stems. It resulted from an earlier sound change of mid vowels to high vowels that took place in words of (c)vcv type when there was a high vowel in the following syllable. This alternation has been obliterated in Modern Kannada as a result of an ensuing grammar-oriented change.

| (3) | *Gloss* | *Old Kannada* | *Modern Kannada* |
|---|---|---|---|
| | he gives | *kuḍuvan* | *koḍutta:ne* |
| | he gave | *koṭṭan* | *koṭṭa* |
| | he enters | *puguvan* | *hogutta:ne* |
| | he entered | *pokkan* | *hokka* |
| | he spoils | *kiḍuvan* | *keḍutta:ne* |
| | he spoiled | *keṭṭan* | *keṭṭa* |

Notice that, in Old Kannada, the verb *kuḍu* 'give', occurring before the present tense suffix, changes to *koṭ* when it is followed by the past tense suffix. In Modern Kannada, it is *koḍu* in the former case and *koṭ* in the latter case. That is, the alternation between the vowels *u* and *o* does not exist in Modern Kannada as *kuḍu* has changed to *koḍu*.

The change of an earlier *u* to *o* and *i* to *e* in the Modern Kannada forms given above is a grammar-oriented change as it affected only the verbs that participated in this alternation. There were certain other words (nouns or adjectives) that were also affected by the earlier sound change. For example, *bisi* 'hot (adj)' alternating with *beccage* 'hot (adv)' or *biḷi* 'white (adj)' alternating with *beḷḷage* 'white (adv)' manifest the effect of that change, and show a comparable morphophonemic alternation. But these were not affected by the latter change. There were also several other isolated words (i.e. words that do not show any morphophonemic alternations) like *idir* 'in front', *iruve* 'ant' which underwent only that earlier sound change. These were also not affected by the latter grammar-oriented change. That is, the latter change was restricted to the verbal paradigm only.

The following pairs of words, belonging to two different dialects of Tulu, exemplify the occurrence of a "sporadic" change of sounds.

| (4) | *Change* | *Gloss* | *Southern* | *Northern* |
|---|---|---|---|---|
| | *ḍ ~ r* | 'belch' | *a:ḍige* | *a:rigɛ* |
| | *g ~ k* | 'stump' | *gutti* | *kutti* |
| | *v ~ d* | 'relative' | *podve* | *podde* |
| | *n ~ ø* | 'fly' | *pa:ntɛ* | *pa:tɛ* |
| | *i ~ i:* | 'here' | *iḍegi* | *i:ḍegi* |
| | *ɛ ~ i* | 'water snake' | *ke:rɛ* | *ke:ri* |

The changes given in (4) are to be regarded as "sporadic" because they have affected only individual words. There are several other words in the language that contain the relevant sounds (like *ḍ, g, v, n, i, e,* etc.) in the relevant environments, but these have not undergone the above-mentioned changes. The conditioning of these changes is therefore lexical and not phonetic.

An example of borrowing affecting the sound system of a language is the following one from Hindi. The sibilant *š* of Sanskrit had become *s* in Prakrit. This continues to be the case in Hindi also, in the case of words that it has inherited from Prakrit. However, Hindi has borrowed several words that contain the sibilant *š* directly from Sanskrit, and in these words, *š* occurs as a distinct sibilant. Thus, borrowing has re-introduced the sound *š* that was lost earlier through a sound change in the history of Hindi.

(5a) *Inherited words in Hindi*:

| *Gloss* | *Sanskrit* | *Prakrit* | *Hindi* |
|---|---|---|---|
| head | *širas* | *sira* | *sir* |

| *Gloss* | *Sanskrit* | *Prakrit* | *Hindi* |
|---|---|---|---|
| school | *ša:la:* | *sa:la* | *sa:l* |
| ten | *daša* | *dasa* | *das* |
| dried | *šuṣka* | *sukkha* | *su:kh* |
| stake | *šu:la* | *su:la* | *su:l* |

(5b) *Borrowed words (directly from Sanskrit) in Hindi*:

| | | | |
|---|---|---|---|
| valiant | *šu:ra* | *su:ra* | *šu:r* |
| destruction | *na:ša* | *ṇa:sa* | *na:š* |
| curse | *ša:pa* | *sa:va* | *ša:p* |
| country | *de:ša* | *de:sa* | *de:š* |
| skilled | *kušala* | *kusala* | *kušal* |

It is necessary to differentiate between sound changes and these additional types of changes that affect sounds because the latter have distinct characteristics of their own. They differ from sound changes (and also from one another) in their motivation, in their effects upon phonological systems, and also in their effects upon the reconstruction of the earlier stages of a language (see 2.4. 1–6 for further details).

Most importantly, sound changes are completely regular from a phonetic point of view. As mentioned earlier, they affect a language at the time in which a new generation of speakers is acquiring its first language. The speakers would generally be unaware of the fact that they are introducing a sound change into their language. They would therefore be incapable of preventing it from applying rather "mechanically" to all the words and affixes that contain the relevant sounds. The change may even destroy some of the most prominent phonological distinctions that occur in the language, and thereby may have devastating effects upon the grammar and lexicon of that language.

Consider the following case of Mysore Kannada. Standard Kannada has a distinction between a series of words that contain an initial *h* and another series that does not contain that sound, as can be seen in the following sets of words:

(6)

| | Standard Kannada | Gloss | Mysore Kannada | Gloss |
|---|---|---|---|---|
| | *ha:ḷu* | 'spoiled' | *a:ḷu* | 'person' |
| | *huḷi* | 'sour' | *uḷi* | 'chisel' |
| | *he:ḷu* | 'say' | *e:ḷu* | 'get up' |
| | *ha:ru* | 'fly' | *a:ru* | 'dry up' |
| | *he:ḍi* | 'timid' | *e:ḍi* | 'crab' |
| | *hakki* | 'bird' | *akki* | 'rice' |
| | *hatti* | 'cotton' | *atti* | 'fig' |
| | *halli* | 'lizard' | *alli* | 'there' |

Notice that the distinction between an initial *h* and its absence is very important for Kannada. The language makes use of this distinction minimally in order to differentiate between several sets of meanings. However, some of the dialects of Kannada, spoken in the Mysore district, have undergone a sound change by which the initial *h* got deleted. As a result, all these pairs of words and several others came to be pronounced in the same way. Words that did not occur in such pairs, but contained an initial *h* also lost that sound. Thus, despite the destructive effect that the sound change had upon the lexicon, its occurrence could not be halted or altered.

The modification of the lexicon that has been caused by a series of changes that affected consonant clusters in the history of Hindi is even more striking (see 7). Consider, for example, the case of medial clusters that contained (a) two different stops or (b) a stop (or nasal) preceded by *r* or *l*. All these clusters were reduced to geminate consonants in Prakrit, with the first consonant becoming identical with the second one. This geminated consonant was later reduced to a single consonant in Hindi.

(7a)

| | Gloss | Sanskrit | Prakrit | Hindi |
|---|---|---|---|---|
| | seven | *sapta* | *satta* | *sa:t* |
| | milk | *dugdha* | *duddha* | *du:dh* |
| | spit out | *udga:ra* | *ugga:la* | *uga:l* |
| | pungent | *tikta* | *titta* | *ti:ta:* |

| | Gloss | Sanskrit | Prakrit | Hindi |
|---|---|---|---|---|
| | cooked rice | *bhata* | *bhatta* | *bha:t* |
| | mung bean | *mudga* | *mugga* | *mũ:g* |
| (7b) | half | *ardha* | *addha* | *a:dh* |
| | rag, cloth | *karpaṭa* | *kappaḍa* | *kapṛa* |
| | dog | *kurkura* | *kukkura* | *ku:kar* |
| | arrogance | *darpa* | *dappa* | *da:p* |
| | leaf | *parṇa* | *paṇṇa* | *pa:n* |
| | work | *karma* | *kamma* | *ka:m* |

The distinctions of meaning that have been affected by these sound changes were of crucial importance in the earlier stage (as, for example, in Sanskrit). There were also several distinctions of grammar that have been completely altered or lost as a result of these changes. We are therefore justified in regarding the changes as devastating. But in spite of this, the speakers of either Prakrit or Hindi were not in a position to prevent these changes from taking place.

Some speakers may become aware of the effects of a sound change after it has taken place in their language. They may then try to undo those effects, as has been happening, for example, in the case of some of the educated speakers of Mysore Kannada. Such efforts, however, do not succeed in reversing the sound change. Instead, they lead to "hypercorrection". That is, modifications would be carried out not only in the case of words that had undergone the earlier change, but also in several others that were not affected by that change. Thus, the educated speakers in Mysore tend to introduce an initial *h* not only in the case of words that contained that sound earlier, but also in the case of words that had only an initial vowel.

| (8) | Gloss | Standard Kannada | Mysore Kannada |
|---|---|---|---|
| | elder sister | *akka* | *hakka* |
| | for this | *idakke* | *hidakke* |

| *Gloss* | *Standard Kannada* | *Mysore Kannada* |
|---|---|---|
| meal | *u:ṭa* | *hu:ṭa* |
| to plough | *uḷu* | *huḷu* |
| there | *alli* | *halli* |

The most important reason why sound changes can have such an impact upon language is that they occur at an unconscious level. We possess two different kinds of knowledge regarding the grammar of our language. One is the knowledge that we acquire when we learn our first language. It is the most crucial one as far as the functioning of our language is concerned, because it forms the basis of our use of the language. However, it occurs at an unconscious level in our brain. We know how to use that knowledge for producing various types of words, word forms and sentences, but we are not aware of the nature of that knowledge. It involves the use of several grammatical rules, but we cannot say what those rules are. We simply "apply" them to words and constructions at the unconscious level.

The second type of knowledge that we possess about the grammar of our language is the one that we acquire in the class while studying books of grammar in school. This is a conscious knowledge. We can describe the rules of grammar that we acquire in this fashion. However, it is not actually needed for speaking or understanding the language. In fact, the uneducated speakers who do not possess any conscious knowledge of this latter type about the grammar of their language, are fluid and competent in their use of the language.

Sound change is a change in pronunciation that affects our unconscious knowledge of grammar. It takes place as a generation of speakers acquires that unconscious knowledge. As it occurs at the unconscious level, speakers are unaware of its occurrence, and therefore have no control over it.

## 1.2 Diachronic and synchronic evidence

Sound change is not readily observable. It needs to be *inferred* from the effects that it leaves behind on the various aspects of language. So we need to examine the various kinds of "evidence" that can be used in order to uncover the sound changes that have taken place in a given language. What are these evidences?

There are two main kinds of evidence that have been used by linguists as the basis of their assumption that one or more sound changes (and also other types of changes) have taken place in a given language. These are derived from diachronic and synchronic comparisons.

(a) *Evidence from diachronic comparison*: If we compare the written records of a language belonging to two different periods in time (like inscriptions), we would find that these records vary from one another on a number of points. These variations are generally considered to represent changes that have taken place in the language from the former period to the later period.

(b) *Evidence from synchronic comparison*: If we compare two geographically adjacent languages that are similar to one another, we would sometimes find that the differences that occur between them have certain definite patterns. It has been argued that the existence of such patterned differences between contemporary languages (or dialects) can be explained by positing a common point (proto-language) from which these languages or dialects have evolved through diachronic processes. This second type of evidence also leads us to the assumption that languages change through time.

There is an interesting difference between these two types of comparisons. Since written records belong to definite periods of time, any changes that we establish on the basis of a comparison of two such records would have a definite temporal direction. For example, a comparison of the records of the eighth and twelfth centuries AD of Kannada indicates that the latter has the consonant *h* in all contexts in which the former has the consonant *p*. Since the former record precedes the latter record in time, we can conclude that the change involved in bringing out this difference is the following:

The consonant *p* of Kannada has become *h* between the eighth and twelfth centuries AD.

A comparison of contemporary dialects or languages, on the other hand, does not provide a similar kind of basis for establishing the direction of change. For example, if we compare two different contemporary dialects of Tulu, namely Shivalli and Sapaliga of Udupi, we find that the latter has the sound *n* in all contexts in which the former has the sound *ṇ* (see (2) in 1.1 for words showing this change). However, there is no evidence here on the basis of which we can determine the direction in which sounds occurring in these dialects have changed. Since both the dialects belong to the same period of time, the difference can be due to any of the following changes affecting the words under consideration:

(i) *ṇ* of Shivalli became *n* in Sapaliga,

(ii) *n* of Sapaliga became *ṇ* in Shivalli, or

(iii) *x* of the proto-language became *n* in Sapaliga and *ṇ* in Shivalli (phonetically, *x* can be any sound that is known to change into a nasal).

Thus, the comparison of dialects or languages belonging to the same period of time cannot provide any "external" means to determine the nature of the change that is responsible for the difference, and also the direction in which the change has taken place. We will need to use some "internal" means for that purpose.

## 1.3 External and internal criteria

One factor that can be used as the basis for establishing the direction of change in the case of synchronic comparisons is the nature of the differences involved. It is possible for some of the phonological *contrasts* that are present in one language to be absent in another language. In such a situation, we can claim that the difference between the two is due to a sound change that has affected the latter language. This claim is based on the hypothesis that phonological contrasts cannot be newly created by sound changes. They can only be obliterated or shifted (see 5.2.1 for details).

For example, in the case of the two Tulu dialects discussed earlier (see (2) in 1.1), there is a distinction between *n* and *ṇ* in Shivalli, which is absent in Sapaliga. The former represents, minimally, a number of meaning distinctions which, however, are not represented by any phonetic distinction in the latter dialect. That is, the relevant words are homonyms in the latter dialect. Since a sound change cannot newly introduce distinctions of the type represented by *n* and *ṇ* in Shivalli, it is possible to claim that the change involved here must be from Shivalli to Sapaliga (i.e. a merger of the two nasals) and not the other way round (see 9).

| (9) | *Gloss* | *Shivalli* | *Sapaliga* |
|---|---|---|---|
| | male | *a:ṇi* | *a:ni* |
| | dine | *uṇi* | *uni* |
| | soil | *maṇṇi* | *manni* |
| | room | *ko:ṇɛ* | *ko:nɛ* |
| | I | *e:ni* | *ya:ni* |
| | wick | *ninɛ* | *ninɛ* |
| | what | *ja:nɛ* | *da:nɛ* |
| | conceiving | *sanɛ* | *tanɛ* |

Another instance of this type can be derived from a comparison of Hindi and Punjabi. In one set of words, Hindi long vowels correspond to Punjabi long vowels, but in another set of words Hindi long vowels correspond to Punjabi short vowels. That is, the contrasts that are represented by the distinction between long and short vowels in Punjabi is absent in Hindi. Since contrasts cannot be newly introduced into a language by a sound change, we can claim that Hindi has lost those contrasts as a result of a sound change, i.e. loss of the vowel length distinction in the words concerned.

A comparison of these sets of words with the corresponding words occurring in Sanskrit indicates that Hindi has lost this distinction in closed syllables (see 10).

| (10) | *Gloss* | *Sanskrit* | *Punjabi* | *Hindi* |
|---|---|---|---|---|
| | thread | *su:tra* | *su:t* | *su:t* |
| | lime | *cu:rṇa* | *cu:nna:* | *cu:na:* |
| | wood | *ka:ṣṭha* | *ka:ṭh* | *ka:ṭhi:* |
| | grape | *dra:kṣa:* | *da:kh* | *da:kh* |
| | stalk | *ka:ṇḍa* | *ka:nna:* | *kã:ṛi:* |

| *Gloss* | *Sanskrit* | *Punjabi* | *Hindi* |
|---|---|---|---|
| work | *ka:rya* | *ka:j* | *ka:j* |
| brush | *ku:rca* | *ku:cca* | *kũ:c* |
| fire | *agni* | *agg* | *a:g* |
| work | *karma* | *kamm* | *ka:m* |
| advice | *šikṣa:* | *sikkh* | *si:kh* |
| son | *putra* | *putt* | *pu:t* |
| friend | *mitra* | *mitt* | *mi:t* |
| milk | *dugdha* | *duddha* | *du:dh* |
| belly | *kukṣi* | *kukkh* | *ku:kh* |

Procedures of the above type can be regarded as making use of an *internal criterion* for determining the direction of sound change. When records belonging to defferent periods in time are being compared as described in the previous section, it involves an *external criterion*. There are drawbacks in the use of either of these two types of criteria for establishing sound changes. It is essential for us to properly examine and understand these drawbacks before making use of these criteria.

Linguists working in this field generally show no hesitation in utilizing the external criterion for establishing sound changes. Only a few scholars have shown their awareness of the pitfalls involved (see Meillet 1967: 23, Hoenigswald 1960: 145), but even in these cases it did not have any appreciable effect upon their reliance on that criterion. This is unfortunate because the external criterion is far less dependable than the internal one as can be seen from the following discussion.

### 1.3.1 LIMITATIONS OF THE EXTERNAL CRITERION

While comparing the written records of a language, belonging to two different periods of time, it is generally taken for granted that the two records follow one another in a straight-line succession. That is, linguists generally "derive", diachronically, the variety of language that occurs in the later record from the one occurring in the earlier record. Thus, the differences existing between two such records are considered to represent historical changes that have taken place in that language between those two periods of time.

This assumption of a straight-line development of a language between two such records is not a necessary one. Even if two distinct records of a language follow one another in time, they may not always represent two distinct "stages" of a language. It is quite possible for the two varieties of the language to be synchronically co-occurring at an earlier stage, with one of them *replacing* the other at a later stage as shown below.

A language community is generally made up of a number of sub-communities, each representing a distinct dialect of its own. This is what we see in various language communities today, and there is no reason why this should not have been the case one or two thousand years earlier. In fact, there must have been more dialectal variety earlier, since the sub-communities would have had less geographical and social contacts, even though this would be partly offset by the fact that the communities were relatively smaller in earlier periods of time.

A community generally selects a speech variety, out of the many existing ones, as the medium for literary creation. This selection would be based upon political, social or economic factors rather than upon linguistic factors. The selected variety would generally represent the speech of the group that is the most active or prominent in the political, literary and cultural fields. As a result, any change in the domination of the political, literary or cultural fields would affect the choice of the language variety that gets used for literary creation. Since the written records that the community leaves behind would be based upon this selected variety, such changes in the choice of the medium for writing would evidently affect the records that the community leaves behind for its posterity.

Thus the history of the written records of a particular language may show shifts in the variety of language that is used from time to time for the purpose of writing as follows (see Meillet 1967):

| | | | | |
|---|---|---|---|---|
| Stage A | 1 | **2** | 3 | 4 |
| Stage B | i | ii | **iii** | iv |
| Stage C | **I** | II | III | IV |
| Stage D | a | b | c | **d** |

Fig. 1. Varieties of speech used for writing

Let us suppose that the variety 2 in Fig. 1 was recorded in stage A, variety iii in stage B, variety I in stage C and variety d in stage D. Notice that in this situation, only the records of the stages B and D represent straight-line developments of the language. Others involve synchronic shifts in the varieties used for recording (i.e. 2 to 3 between stages A and B, III to I between stages B to C and I to IV between stages C and D), in addition to diachronic changes that have affected the language.

Figure 1 represents what is most probably the normal situation in the recorded history of languages. That is, the difference between two different written records of a language, belonging to two different periods of time, would generally represent a combination of diachronic change and synchronic (dialectal) shift. Hence, the use of external evidence for establishing the nature and direction of sound change is extremely hazardous.

For example, supposing that the stages A and B in Fig. 1 differ in that the consonant *s* of stage A corresponds to the consonant *š* of stage B. The proponents of a straight-line succession hypothesis would posit a sound change of the following nature unhesitatingly as an explanation for this difference:

*s* of A became *š* in B.

As can be seen from Fig. 1, on the other hand, the difference between the stages A and B (as shown by the two records 2 and iii respectively that have been preserved), is in fact a combination of the differences between (a) the varieties 2 and 3 of the same period, and (b) between 3 and iii of different periods. Thus, it is possible that the above difference occurring between records 2 and iii (namely that the consonant *s* of record 2 corresponds to the consonant *š* of record iii) actually represents a synchronic difference which had existed in stage A itself between its two varieties, namely 2 and 3. It might just be an accident that only variety 2, and not variety 3, was represented in the records of stage A that have been preserved. And in such an event, the change involved could be any of the following:

(i) *s* of A became *š* in B, or

(ii) *š* of the earlier stage became *s* in A, but remained as *š* in B, or even

(iii) *x* (an unknown sound) became *s* in A and *š* in B.

Thus, the difference between two successive written records of a language can have two different explanations. The difference may be due to (i) certain diachronic changes that took place between the two recorded stages, or (ii) a shift in the dialect that came into use for the purpose of writing during the second stage. In the former case, external evidence can be used as the basis for establishing the direction of change, but in the latter case that evidence is completely useless for that purpose. It is actually misleading in the latter case.

The known histories of Indian languages provide interesting instances of shifts of this type in the dialects that were used for writing and other literary purposes. For example, it has been suggested that Vedic Sanskrit is based upon a north-western dialect, whereas Classical Sanskrit is based upon a central dialect. That is, differences occurring between Vedic Sanskrit and Classical Sanskrit need not necessarily be derived through changes from the former to the latter. Scholars have also adduced linguistic evidence in support of a claim that Prakrit also does not derive directly from Sanskrit.

Another situation of this type occurs in the history of Kannada. There have been possibly several shifts in the use of social and geographical dialects for the purpose of writing in this language. For example, Old Kannada represents primarily the writings of Jaina authors, whereas Middle Kannada represents primarily the writings of Virashaiva authors. The former is probably a southern dialect and the latter a northern dialect. Modern Standard Kannada, on the other hand, has apparently seen another shift to the south, as it is more similar to the spoken variety of the south (Mysore) than that of the north. It would therefore be a mistake to assume that three different written records, belonging to these three varieties of Kannada (called Old, Middle and Modern), represent three diachronic stages of its history.

The value of external evidence is further reduced by the fact that the effects of dialectal shift and diachronic change on written records are practically identical. Their occurrence in the history of such records is also unpredictably mixed up. One may try to predict the occurrence of dialectal shift in certain special contexts on the basis of known political or cultural upheavals, but since such upheavals need not necessarily lead to shifts in the literary medium, the validity of predictions based upon them is very much reduced.

It is necessary to specifically take note of the above-mentioned limitation of the external criterion. A number of generalizations regarding sound change, such as its spread, tendency towards maximum utilization of rules, markedness theory, direction of occurrence, and many others have been based upon conclusions that have been derived on the basis of the external criterion. The validity of these generalizations is clearly questionable because of the doubtful validity of external evidence.

Another interesting point is that written records of earlier stages are available only for a small number of languages that are currently in use in the world. There is only synchronic evidence for the majority of the languages of the world. We are therefore forced to depend upon synchronic evidence while trying to understand the sound changes that have affected the majority of the world's languages.

### 1.3.2 INTERNAL CRITERIA: DESCRIPTIVE EVIDENCE

There are two different aspects of language that can provide the basis for internal criteria, namely descriptive evidence and comparative evidence. Both these have been used for postulating sound changes. Descriptive evidence is derived by the descriptive study of individual languages, while comparative evidence is derived by the comparison of two or more different languages or dialects. Descriptive evidence is based on certain specific properties of the language under study. These properties specify the linguistic changes that were integrated into that grammar. The comparative evidence, on the other hand, is based upon certain specific types of differences that exist between the two languages being compared. These differences tell the linguist what specific diachronic processes have brought them into existence.

The principle underlying the use of descriptive evidence is the assumption that the synchronic stage of a language is mostly the outcome of diachronic processes that have been affecting the language during the past many thousands of years (Greenberg 1966). For example, if a language shows a morphophonemic alternation between two sounds, it can be assumed that there was only one sound instead of the two alternating ones at an earlier stage. We can assume further that the sound split into two different sounds and thereby gave rise to the morphophonemic alternation.

We can exemplify the use of this principle with the help of the following example from Marathi. There is a morphophonemic alternation in this language between alveolar and palatal affricates *c* and *č* with the latter occurring before *i*, *y* and the former elsewhere. The alternation occurs in the number-gender paradigm of some of the possessive pronouns as in (11):

| (11) | *Gloss* | *Masculine Singular* | *Masculine Plural* | *Feminine Singular* | *Feminine Plural* |
|---|---|---|---|---|---|
| | his | *tyaca* | *tyace* | *tyačī* | *tyačya* |
| | her | *tica* | *tice* | *tičī* | *tičya* |
| | our | *amca* | *amce* | *amčī* | *amčya* |
| | your | *tumca* | *tumce* | *tumčī* | *tumčya* |
| | their | *tyanca* | *tyance* | *tyančī* | *tyančya* |

We can claim that there was no morphophonemic alternation corresponding to the above one earlier and further that the words had the same consonant in both the forms. We can derive the alternation by postulating a conditioned change of that consonant. In the present case, it was the change of *c* to *č* before *i* and *y* that has given rise to this morphophonemic alternation.

Another example can be that of Hindi, in which we find nasalized vowels occurring in certain words like *gã:ṭh* 'knot', *dã:t* 'tooth', *pã:c* 'five', *cã:d* 'moon', etc. in which there is no neighbouring nasal that can induce nasalization. We can assume that the language had a nasal consonant in all these words. We can assume further that the language had lost that nasal at some stage, but the nasalization that it had induced upon the neighbouring vowel has remained (Ferguson 1966). The internal evidence here is based upon the nature of sounds. In this particular case of Hindi, there is supporting evidence from Sanskrit, a language belonging to an earlier period of time, and hence providing external evidence:

| (12a) | *Gloss* | *Sanskrit* | *Hindi* |
|---|---|---|---|
| | smoke | *dhu:ma* | *dhu:ã* |
| | tooth | *danta* | *dã:t* |
| | moon | *candra* | *cã:d* |
| | five | *pañca* | *pã:c* |
| | thread | *tantu* | *tã:t* |
| | thorn | *kaṇṭaka* | *kã:ṭ* |

There would be some exceptions to generalizations of this latter type because they are not as dependable as those of the former type. Hindi itself provides exceptional cases for the generalization regarding nasalization. That is, Hindi shows nasalization in words like *sã:p* 'snake' (from Sanskrit *sarpa*), *ã:su:* 'tears' (from Sanskrit *ašru*), etc., in which there was not any earlier nasal. Despite such exceptions, the assumptions generally hold well.

| (12b) | *Gloss* | *Sanskrit* | *Hindi* |
|---|---|---|---|
| | snake | *sarpa* | *sã:p* |
| | tears | *ašru* | *ã:su:* |
| | high | *ucca* | *ũ:c* |
| | eye | *akši* | *ã:kh* |
| | camel | *uṣṭra* | *ũ:ṭh* |

How do we arrive at these specific properties of language that can be used for inferring the underlying diachronic processes? One of the main tasks of the linguist here is to separate the universal properties of a language from those that are non-universal in their distribution. Only the latter can form the basis for inferring the diachronic processes that are undergone by the language. Universal properties, by definition, cannot be the result of diachronic processes, unless they are universal only by accident (i.e. really non-universal).

Non-universal properties, on the other hand, are to be derived through changes that occurred in the language some time in the past. Because they are non-universal in their occurrence it is possible to think that they have been lost, gained, or altered in a given language. An examination of non-universal properties indicates that some, such as the occurrence of nasalized vowels in Hindi, readily indicate the exact diachronic process that could have introduced them into the language. (Nasalized vowels have been considered to derive from the loss of neighbouring nasals.) There are other properties, however, that can have more than one source of derivation. The voiced bilabial stops, for example, can be derived from voiceless bilabial stops, voiced bilabial continuants, or even from voiced bilabial nasals. In these latter instances, the exact change involved cannot be arrived at with the help of the particular property alone.

Thus, the second important task of the linguist is to establish the possible diachronic sources of various non-universal properties occurring in different languages. He can arrive at these sources through detailed studies of individual properties from the point of view of languages with known history, and thereby establish universal diachronic rules, such as the one regarding nasalized vowels mentioned above.

The so-called "known histories" of languages are actually based upon external (and partly internal) evidence and hence, their use in deriving diachronic universals that would later on form the basis for internal evidence must be carried out with utmost care. We must not forget that all the limitations of external evidence pointed out above get transferred automatically to the diachronic universals that are established in that fashion. There are cases of language histories that have been partly based on internal criteria, such as gradualness hypothesis or the hypothesis of economy or simplification of rules. Diachronic universals derived on the basis of such histories of languages would simply be the result of circular inferences and would therefore be worthless.

There are also certain synchronic aspects of language, called implicational universals, that can be used directly for establishing diachronic universals. For example, a particular type of consonants, called implosives, occur in a number of American Indian languages, and also in a fairly large number of African and south-east Asian languages. In India, for example, they occur in Sindhi and Gujarati. A study of these languages indicates that there are no languages that have only back implosives but no front implosives. This finding can form the basis of an implicational universal, namely that the presence of back implosives implies the presence of front implosives (Greenberg 1971: 303).

If this implicational universal is correct, then any diachronic process that one postulates regarding the occurrence of implosives as having taken place in the history of a language should have as its starting point as well as its ending point a synchronic state that satisfies the above-mentioned universal statement. That is, one cannot postulate a diachronic process that ends in (or has to start from) a synchronically unlawful state. If any two properties are implicationally related in all known languages of the world, there is no justification to believe that they were not so earlier, or that they would not retain that relationship at a later stage.

Such implicational universals, being based upon the actual observation of the distribution of various language properties, are unaffected by the limitations of external evidence mentioned earlier. They are therefore more dependable than the other criteria, especially when they are used for verifying diachronic processes that have already been established on some other basis (such as the external criteria).

### 1.3.3 INTERNAL CRITERIA: COMPARATIVE EVIDENCE

The use of comparative evidence for establishing diachronic processes is based on the genetic hypothesis. According to this hypothesis, similarities between two compared languages can in many instances be explained, especially if the similarities are pervasive and deep rooted, by assuming that the two languages have inherited them from a common ancestral language. That is, such languages are assumed to be the continuations of a single language, belonging to an earlier period, with the continuation taking two distinct directions, and thereby causing a language split.

The above hypothesis does not claim that a genetic explanation is the only possible explanation for the occurrence of similarities between two languages. Certain other factors could also possibly be the basis of similarities. For example, one of the two languages might have borrowed heavily from the other language, and this might be the cause of the similarities occurring between them. It is also possible for certain similarities to derive from the fact that the feature under consideration is a language universal one. There can also be accidental similarities between two languages. Hence, it is not just the similarity that forms the basis of genetic relationship, but similarity that is pervasive and deep-rooted.

A problem with regard to the genetic explanation is that the cause of a given resemblance cannot be easily determined. That is, resemblances do not contain any indication as to what has caused them. The same type of resemblance can result from inheritance, borrowing or accidental similarity. Moreover, resemblances resulting from genetic relationship (inheritance) generally pervade the whole of basic vocabulary and grammar to the extent that no other resemblance is found to pervade. But such quantitative factors cannot be used as defining criteria.

Thus, the genetic hypothesis is incapable of providing any means for distinguishing between resemblances resulting from inheritance on the one hand, and from borrowing, convergence, and such other factors on the other. This is a limitation of the hypothesis. However, it does provide a procedure for evaluating the assumption of genetic relationship, once it has been postulated on the basis of similarities that exist between the two languages. The procedure is based upon the principle that differences that occur between two genetically related languages must necessarily be explainable with the help of diachronic changes that one or both of them have undergone from the time they constituted a single language to the present.

Thus, the assumption that two different languages are genetically related can be verified by reconstructing the ancestral language that is common to both of them. It must be possible to derive each of the languages from that common ancestral language (proto-language) through the postulation of a series of diachronic processes. A similar type of explanation would not be available in the case of languages that have become similar to one another due to borrowing. Even if two such languages have become very similar to one another, the differences that occur between them, especially in their basic structure and vocabulary, would be such that they cannot have been derived from a single source.

The best verification for the genetic hypothesis is available in the comparison of dialects where the difference involved is very small. Only a few simple diachronic processes need to be postulated to show that the two are derived from a single source. In the comparison of languages that are more distinct from one another, on the other hand, the number of differences that need to be explained would be numerous. Many of them might resist any attempt to explain them. The crucial point is that the validity of an assumption of genetic relationship between two languages would depend upon the amount of differences that can be explained by postulating diachronic processes, rather than upon the amount of similarities that can be discovered as occurring between them. Linguists who write about the relationship between languages generally miss this crucial point about genetic hypothesis.

The value of genetic hypothesis as an internal criterion for postulating sound changes is very clear. It makes it essential for the various assumptions of sound change that have been postulated in connection with the history of a given language to form a unified system of changes. It also makes it necessary for these changes to fit in with various other changes that have been postulated for deriving other related languages such that the whole series of changes postulated for the history of the whole family form a unified system of changes. Thus, the hypothesis brings systematicity into the study of sound change.

It is interesting to note that the comparison of written records belonging to two different periods of time can also provide comparative evidence that can be used for postulating sound changes. However, the changes postulated in this fashion can easily conflict with changes that we postulate by using the records as forming external evidence. In the case of such conflicts, the former procedure is more reliable than the latter procedure.

## 1.4 SUMMARY

Sound change is a change in the pronunciation of sounds. It takes place at an unconscious level as a generation of speakers is acquiring its first language. It is conditioned only by phonetic factors, and not by other factors such as the function of sounds in a language, their relevance to grammar or meaning, prestige of speakers, etc. It is also free of any interference from the speakers of a language, as it occurs at the unconscious level.

The effects that a sound change produces on the sounds of a language can be altered at a later stage by other types of changes that occur in the language, such as grammar-oriented changes, borrowings and sporadic changes.

Sound change is not directly observable. Its occurrence has to be inferred on the basis of the effect that it leaves behind on the sounds of a language. There are two kinds of evidence that can be used for this purpose, (i) diachronic and (ii) synchronic. Diachronic evidence is derived from a comparison of two sets of records of a language that belong to two different periods of time. Synchronic evidence, on the other hand, is derived either (a) from the descriptive study of a given language or (b) from the comparison of two or more dialects or languages that belong to the same period of time.

The two types of evidence differ from one another in that the diachronic evidence provides a basis (called external criterion), namely the relative age of the two sets of records that are compared, for determining the direction in which the changes have taken place. No such basis is available in the case of the synchronic evidence. This basis, however, is not very reliable because there can be shifts in the dialect used for the purpose of creating those records.

There is, on the other hand, a more reliable basis for determining the nature and direction of change, the internal criterion. This is provided by descriptive as well as comparative studies of languages. In the former case, one can examine the properties of a language and postulate that some of those properties derive from changes that had taken place earlier in that language. Such postulations, which depend upon the nature of those properties, can be regarded as making use of descriptive evidence. In the latter case, on the other hand, one can study the differences that occur between the two languages compared, and establish changes that account for those differences. This is necessary if one has to assume that the two languages or dialects derive from one single proto-language (i.e. they were identical at an earlier stage). Such postulations of changes can be regarded as making use of comparative evidence.

In the case of a conflict between external and internal criteria, the internal criterion should be selected because it is more reliable than external criterion.

## FURTHER READINGS

1. Regarding the evaluation of evidence, see
   Goyvaerts 1975. *Present-day historical and comparative linguistics,* ch. 1.
   Anderson 1973. *Structural aspects of language change,* ch. 1.
   Lehmann 1963. *Historical linguistics,* ch. 4.
   Bloomfield 1933. *Language,* ch. 17.
   Wrenn 1943. *The value of spelling as evidence.*
2. Regarding the kinds of evidence, see
   Meillet 1967. *Comparative method in historical linguistics.*

# 2

# CHARACTERISTICS OF SOUND CHANGE

## 2.1 Introduction

In this chapter, we will examine the characteristics of sound change. These will help us to identify sound change and also to differentiate them from other types of changes that affect sounds in a language, such as analogy or grammar-oriented changes, sporadic changes and changes resulting from the borrowing of words from other languages or dialects. The most important characteristics that have been assigned to sound change are their regularity and irreversibility. It is true that several linguists have questioned the correctness of these two characteristics, but as we will see, most of their objections derive from a mix up of sound changes with other types of changes that affect sounds in a language like analogy and borrowing.

Sound changes are also considered to have a definite direction of occurrence. Given the type of sound that is changing and the type of phonetic environment that is causing that change, it would generally be possible to predict the type of sound change that is going to take place. However, we are not in a position to say whether or not a predicted sound change is going to take place in a given language. Nor are we in a position to say when such a change, if at all, is going to take place. That is, we can only predict the direction of sound change, but not its time or location. This ability to predict the direction of sound change is yet to be properly developed. We have yet to gather the necessary typological detail that can form the basis of such predictions.

## 2.2 MECHANISM OF SOUND CHANGE

As explained in chapter 1, sound changes can affect our language rather "mechanically" and in a completely regular fashion. Only phonetic or physiological factors can influence and constrain their occurrence. Sound changes can make our grammar very complex by introducing several morphophonemic alternations. They can even be devastating for the grammar and the lexicon as they can destroy many of the important distinctions that occur in them. They have this power mainly because they occur at the unconscious level. We have no conscious control over them.

As pointed out in the previous chapter we possess two kinds of knowledge about the grammar of our language—one occurs at the conscious level and the other at the unconscious level. The knowledge that we acquire when we learn our first language is an unconscious one. It occurs probably in the form of a neural network in our brain, which when activated triggers the muscles in our vocal tract to automatically activate and as a result, we produce the necessary words and sentences. However, we only have the ability to make use of this unconscious knowledge for producing and understanding speech. We do not have the ability to consciously observe that knowledge or its usage. That is, we know how to use it, but we do not know what it is that we use or how we use it. The knowledge occurs and also functions at the unconscious level.

The second type of knowledge that we possess about the grammar of our language is a conscious one. We acquire this knowledge in our classes by studying the grammar textbooks or by analysing the words and sentences that occur in our language. We are in a position to describe that knowledge as consisting of several grammatical rules of different types. We are also able to apply those rules consciously to words and affixes and produce not only sentences but also paradigms of different kinds. We can conjugate verbs or provide different case forms of nouns or pronouns. However, compared to the unconscious knowledge of grammar, this conscious knowledge is very limited and incomplete. It may even be incorrect as a grammar or description of our language.

We have the ability to possess such two-fold systems of knowledge in the case of our other bodily functions as well. Consider, for example, the "knowledge" that we possess about the way in which we manipulate our eyes. We can see things that are very near to us, and also things that are far away from us. We can see stable things, and also things that are moving. We need to move our eyeballs in many ways in order to do this. We know how to do this, but we do not know how we do it. That is, our knowledge about the way in which we move our eyeballs occurs at an unconscious level. However, an ophthalmologist, who has studied these various aspects of the eye and has conducted several experimental studies, has a conscious knowledge of those movements. He can describe how they take place and how a human being is able to control those movements. Notice, however, that this conscious knowledge is not as complete as the unconscious knowledge. There are still several "gray" areas that the ophthalmologist is not very sure of. His conscious knowledge may also be partly incorrect.

Sound change is a change in the pronunciation of sounds. It affects the unconscious knowledge of grammar as a generation of speakers is acquiring that knowledge. Since it takes place at the unconscious level, speakers are incapable of perceiving it or controlling it, and hence they are also incapable of preventing it from taking place. This is why sound change can be extremely regular, and can have devastating effects upon the grammar and the lexicon of a language (see 1.1).

There are several points that support the claim that sound change affects a language when a generation of speakers is acquiring it as its first language. The following are three important points in this regard.

### 2.2.1 GAP IN THE CONTINUITY OF LANGUAGE

The only period in which there is a gap in the continuity of language is when it is being transferred from one generation to another, i.e. when a new generation of speakers is acquiring it from adult speakers. Since sound changes can be devastating in their effects upon language, this gap is the ideal place to situate them. Adults do not "teach" the language to their children. They merely speak in it with their children just as they speak in it with other members of the family. Thus, children acquire the knowledge of the language by merely being exposed to it. Hence, there is a greater possibility for the pronunciation of sounds to get altered at this stage than at any later stage when the children grow up and use that language in their daily life.

Generations are considered to be discrete in the case of a family, but continuous in the case of a community. We, therefore, have to assume that the discreteness that occurs in individual families forms the basis of sound changes. This means that in spite of the continuity of different generations in a community as a whole, the discreteness that separates them from one another in individual families can be strong enough to form the basis for sound changes. This claim is supported by the reports of certain sound changes that appear to separate generations among communities.

One such situation has been reported to occur in the Havyaka dialect of Kannada spoken in Puttur, South Kanara. Adults of this community have a *y*-glide after words that end in *i* or *e*, and a *w*-glide after words that end in *a*, when those words are followed by an emphatic suffix (see 1). Children, on the other hand, have been found to use a *w*-glide in the case of both these types of words.

| (1) | *Words* | *Gloss* | *Emphatic forms* | |
|---|---|---|---|---|
| | | | *Adults* | *Children* |
| | *abbe* | 'mother' | *abbey-e:* | *abbew-e:* |
| | *mane* | 'house' | *maney-e:* | *manew-e:* |
| | *kutti* | 'stump' | *kuttiy-e:* | *kuttiw-e:* |
| | *di:pa* | 'lamp | *di:paw-e:* | *di:paw-e:* |
| | *dappa* | 'thick' | *dappaw-e:* | *dappaw-e:* |
| | *bi:ga* | 'lock' | *bi:gaw-e:* | *bi:gaw-e:* |

It is evident that communities tolerate such differences when they occur in the speech of their children, in exactly the same manner in which they tolerate other cultural differences that together form the generation gap.

### 2.2.2 ORDER OF ACQUISITION

The order in which children acquire the distinctions of sounds that are necessary for their language is in agreement with some of the implicational universals that have been postulated by linguists. For example, a child acquires stops before acquiring fricatives. This order is in agreement with the fact that the occurrence of fricatives in a language implies the occurrence of stops in it. That is, if there are one or more fricatives in a language, we expect it to have at least some stops. Similarly, a child acquires front consonants before acquiring the respective back consonants. It acquires a *p*, for example, before acquiring a *k* (as part of its speech). This is also in agreement with the implicational universal that the presence of back consonants implies the presence of front consonants.

Distinctions that occur more frequently in the various languages of the world are acquired early by the child, whereas the ones that are less frequent are acquired rather late. For example, the distinction between *l* and *r* occurs less frequently in languages than the distinction between *p* and *t*. Children acquire the latter distinction earlier than the former one. As I will be pointing out later (see 2.6), these implicational universals are also connected with the types of sound changes that occur in language. For example, they do not appear to produce phonological systems that go against these implicational universals. That is, they do not appear to give rise to synchronically non-existing types of languages.

### 2.2.3 MUTATIONS IN THE ACQUISITION

Sound changes that have been postulated for various languages of the world are strikingly parallel to "mutations" that occur when children are acquiring the language. If we consider sound changes as primarily the stabilizations and continuations of such mutations, we can not only account for the parallelism between the two, but also provide a mechanism for sound change.

Children acquire the distinctions that are specific to their language gradually through binary splitting. The consonant *t*, which represented *k* and *t* at one stage, for example, would be split into two. The trill *r*, which represented *r* and *l* earlier, would then be divided into two, and so on. Such binary splits are induced by the existence of the relevant distinctions in the adult speech to which the children are exposed. It is conceivable that during this process of gradual acquisition, children may fail to achieve their goal in any of the following three ways, thereby acquiring an unconscious knowledge of grammar that is different from the grammar of the adult speakers.

(i) They may fail to acquire a distinction that existed in the adult speech as a relevant (contrastive) or irrelevant (non-contrastive) distinction. This can lead to the merger of two sounds. The loss of the *ṇ~n* contrast in the Sapagaliga dialect of Tulu, described earlier [see (2) of 1.1], could have developed in this way. Another example is the loss of the distinction between the sounds *s*, *š* and *ṣ* in Middle Indo-Aryan [see (5) of 1.1].

(ii) They may acquire a new distinction that did not exist in the adult speech. That is, the binary splitting may continue even after the children have acquired all the necessary distinctions. The distinction derived from the split may only be an irrelevant (non-contrastive) one to begin with, but it may become relevant (contrastive) as a result of later changes. For example, vowels occurring before nasals may get nasalized. The distinction between oral and nasalized vowels that gets introduced into the language as a result of this change, however, would remain irrelevant as long as the nasals remain in tact. When the nasals get deleted following a sound change, the distinction between oral vowels and nasalized vowels would become contrastive. Another example can be the development of tonal distinction in Punjabi, described in the next section.

(iii) They may replace an existing relevant distinction by an irrelevant distinction that might have existed simultaneously in the adult speech. For example, Punjabi has undergone a sound change by which initial voiced aspirates were de-aspirated and made voiceless. This change had the effect of removing, from the language, the distinction between initial voiced aspirates and initial voiceless unaspirates. Prior to this change, however, the language must have developed a tonal distinction in the vowels that followed the aspirates, such that the vowels were in low tone after voiced aspirates and in high tone after voiceless unaspirates. When the distinction between voiced aspirates and voiceless unaspirates was lost, the contrast that was represented by it earlier shifted to the tonal distinction, and as a result, it became relevant.

(2a) *High tone after voiceless unaspirates*:

| *Gloss* | *Sanskrit* | *Punjabi* |
|---|---|---|
| bitter | *kaṭuka* | *koṛa:* |
| work | *karma* | *kamm* |
| wood | *ka:ṣṭha* | *ka:ṭh* |
| thread | *tantu* | *tand* |

(2b) *Low tone after voiced aspirates that became voiceless unaspirates*:

| | | |
|---|---|---|
| horse | *ghoṭaka* | *kòṛa:* |
| thick | *ghana* | *kàṇa:* |
| pitcher | *ghaṭa* | *kàṛa:* |
| wealth | *dhana* | *tàn* |

These different parallels occurring between the aspects of child language and sound change make it possible to claim that sound change occurs at the acquisitional stage of language.

## 2.3 Regularity hypothesis

During the second half of the nineteenth century, a group of linguists, who came to be known later on as Neogrammarians (or Young Grammarians), put forth an exciting hypothesis regarding the nature of sound change called the "Regularity Hypothesis." They claimed that sound changes are very different from other language changes in that they operate mechanically and regularly without any exceptions. That is, sound changes can only be conditioned by phonetic factors and not by grammatical, lexical or semantic factors. The postulation of this very strong hypothesis concerning the nature of sound change completely revolutionized the study of the diachronic or historical aspects of language. It made that study highly systematic.

There have been severe criticisms of this hypothesis, but two important generalizations that formed the basis of the hypothesis appear to have stood the test of time. They are concerned with (i) the regularity of sound change, and (ii) the irreversibility of sound change.

### 2.3.1 REGULARITY OF SOUND CHANGE

Sound changes are considered to be regular in that they affect the whole paradigm of the sounds involved. As such, they can only be conditioned by phonetic factors. That is, sound changes directly affect sounds and not individual words. They affect words only indirectly because of the fact that the sounds that changed had occurred in those words.

Consider, for example, the change of Sanskrit *š* to *s* in Prakrit. It is a change in the pronunciation of the two sounds. The speakers of the language at an earlier stage were able to produce three different sibilants - *s*, *š* and *ṣ*). But at a particular period in the history of that language, they stopped differentiating between *s* and *š*, and started using only one sibilant, namely *s*. As a result of this change, every single word that earlier contained the sound *š* now came to be pronounced with the sound *s* (see 3).

| (3) | *Gloss* | *Sanskrit* | *Prakrit* |
|---|---|---|---|
| | lake | *saras* | *sara* |
| | arrow | *šara* | *sara* |
| | seven | *sapta* | *satta* |
| | able | *šakta* | *satta* |
| | all | *sarva* | *savva* |
| | corpse | *šava* | *savva* |
| | lead | *si:sa* | *si:sa* |
| | conduct | *ši:la* | *si:la* |

As discussed earlier, changes of this type take place at the acquisitional stage of a language. When a new generation of speakers acquired an earlier form of Prakrit (a kind of Old Prakrit), they failed to acquire the distinction between the two sibilants, and as a result, the sound change got introduced into their speech. Since it was a change in the pronunciation of the relevant sounds, and not of the words in which the sounds occurred as such, its effect on those words was complete. That is, irrespective of the meaning or importance of individual words, the change affected all of them uniformly. In Prakrit, for example, even the most important meaning distinctions (important from the point of view of the earlier stage, namely Sanskrit) have been lost as a result of this change (along with certain other sound changes), as can be seen from the pairs of words mentioned earlier.

Another interesting observation that supports the regularity hypothesis is that sound changes that affect a sound only partially (i.e. conditioned sound changes) leave behind morphophonemic alternations that make the grammar of the language even more complex. For example, Sanskrit had undergone, at an earlier stage, a merger of two sounds, *t* and *d* in the word-final position. The two sounds, however, were kept distinct in other positions like word-initial and intervocal. As a result, stems that contained a final *d* came to show two different forms, (i) with a final *t* when no suffix followed them, and (ii) with a final *d* when a suffix with an initial vowel followed them (see 4a). These alternating forms contrast with forms that do not show any comparable alternation because they already possessed a final *t* that was *t* even when a suffix with an initial vowel followed (see 4b).

| | *Nominative* | *Gloss* | *Instrumental* | *Gloss* |
|---|---|---|---|---|
| (4a) | *šarat* | 'autumn' | *šarad-a:* | 'by autumn' |
| | *sampat* | 'wealth' | *sampad-a:* | 'by wealth' |
| | *vipat* | 'calamity' | *vipad-a:* | 'by calamity' |
| (4b) | *marut* | 'wind' | *marut-a:* | 'by wind' |
| | *sarit* | 'river' | *sarit-a:* | 'by river' |
| | *jagat* | 'world' | *jagat-a:* | 'by world' |

It must be conceded, however, that the regularity occurring in the effects of a given sound change can be disturbed by changes that take place later in that language. Borrowings from a neighbouring language or from earlier records of the same language can introduce words that contain the lost sound in the relevant environments. For example, Kannada has completely changed an initial *p* to *h* probably in the ninth century AD. It later borrowed words like *pu:rva* 'east', *pa:pa* 'sin', *paṭṭaṇa* 'city', etc. from Sanskrit. Kannada also borrowed words like *pa:ḍu* 'suffering', *paḍe* 'army', *peṭṭu* 'beating', *pitta* 'bile', etc. from its own earlier stage. These now appear as exceptions to the regularity of the change of initial *p* to *h*. We find another example in Hindi in which the regularity of the effects of an earlier *s-š* merger has been disturbed by borrowings from Sanskrit (see 5 of 1.1).

It is also possible for certain grammar-oriented changes to alter the effects of a sound change, and thereby make it appear that it might have been conditioned by grammatical or lexical factors. For example, Old Kannada had undergone a change of *o* to *u* (and also *e* to *i*) when that vowel was followed by a single consonant and a high vowel (*i* or *u*). This change appears to have taken place in the seventh or eight century AD. It had affected both nominal as well as verbal stems, but in the latter case this change has given rise to the introduction of a morphophonemic alternation in the case of verbs that were of the (c)vc*u* type, as can be seen in the following sets of forms:

(5a) *Old Kannada forms*

| *Non-past form* | *Gloss* | *Past form* | *Gloss* |
|---|---|---|---|
| *kuḍu-van* | 'he will give' | *koṭ-ṭan* | 'he gave' |
| *tuḍu-van* | 'he will wear' | *toṭ-ṭan* | 'he wore' |
| *pugu-van* | 'he will enter' | *pok-kan* | 'he entered' |

Notice that these verbal bases have two different stems each, one with the vowel *u* in the initial syllable and the other with the vowel *o* in the same position. (The latter form also shows additional differences like loss of the final vowel and devoicing of the penultimate stop.) This alternation has resulted from the fact that the vowel *o* was followed by *u* in the non-past form, but by *a* in the past form. The change of *o* to *u* has also affected several other words, including verbal bases, but these did not participate in the above-mentioned alternation.

In the case of Modern Kannada, on the other hand, verbs of the above type show the vowel *o* in both the non-past and past tenses. That is, the verbs do not show the *u~o* alternation and are, therefore, similar to other verbs of the (c)vc*u* type.

(5b) *Modern Kannada forms*

| *Non-past form* | *Gloss* | *Past form* | *Gloss* |
|---|---|---|---|
| *koḍu-tta:ne* | 'he gives' | *koṭ-ṭa* | 'he gave' |
| *hogu-tta:ne* | 'he enters' | *hok-ka* | 'he entered' |
| *toḍu-tta:ne* | 'he wears' | *toṭ-ṭa* | 'he wore' |
| *biḍu-tta:ne* | 'he leaves' | *biṭ-ṭa* | 'he left' |
| *iḍu-tta:ne* | 'he places' | *iṭ-ṭa* | 'he placed' |
| *nagu-tta:ne* | 'he laughs' | *nak-ka* | 'he laughed' |

However, Modern Kannada retains the effects of the earlier sound change in the case of other verbs such as *kudi* 'boil', *tuḷi* 'kick', *suli* 'peel', etc. It also retains the effects in the case of words belonging to other categories such as *huḍi* 'powder', *turike* 'itch', etc. The latter may involve even a morphophonemic alternation as can be seen in the pair *tudi* 'tip': *toṭṭu* 'stem'. That is, when examined from the point of view of Modern Kannada, the change appears to be conditioned by a morphological distinction. However, it is possible to claim that Modern Kannada has undergone a grammar-oriented change that removed the effects of the earlier sound change in the case of verbs of the type (c)vc*u*, and thereby made the grammar less complex, but at the same time made the effects of earlier sound change less revealing.

### 2.3.2 IRREVERSIBILITY OF SOUND CHANGE

The second generalization connected with the regularity hypothesis is that sound changes are irreversible. Once a sound change has taken place, its effects upon grammar and lexicon are so numerous and scattered that it cannot be reversed through any of the following sound changes or other types of language changes. It might be possible to bring back into the language some of the lexical distinctions that have been lost by such changes, as for example, by borrowing words from neighbouring dialects or from earlier stages of the same language. However, these cannot be considered as reversals of earlier sound changes. The point to be noted here is that the earlier changes would have effected not only words in which the sound under consideration is minimally contrastive, but also several other words.

Similarly, grammar-oriented changes may remove from a language morphophonemic alternations that have been introduced into it by earlier sound changes as has been mentioned earlier. It is also possible for the direction of these later changes to be exactly opposite to that of the earlier sound changes, as has apparently happened in the case of the above-mentioned grammar-oriented change in Modern Kannada. However, since such changes remove only some of the effects that have been left behind by the original sound change, these cannot be considered as "reversals" of that change.

As I will be pointing out later, this claim concerning the irreversibility of sound changes is of utmost importance for the theory of linguistic reconstruction. Some of the most important and startling results attained by the comparative method in historical linguistics are based upon this assumption. In fact, the main basis of the comparative method, namely the assumption that lost sets of oppositions cannot be brought back into a language through following sound changes (or other types of language changes) is a conclusion drawn from this irreversibility hypothesis (see 4.2.3 for details).

### 2.3.3 ABSENCE OF SHARP BOUNDARIES

The most consistent criticism that has been levelled against the regularity hypothesis has come from dialectologists. Their arguments are mainly based upon the fact that dialect studies do not confirm any of the corollaries that can be derived from the regularity hypothesis. For example, the hypothesis makes one expect that a dialect study would show sharp and clear-cut boundaries between two different dialects, of which one has undergone a given sound change and the other one has not. However, a number of dialect studies conducted in different parts of the world report that the boundaries between two such pairs of dialects appear to be rather vague, hazy and confusing Hence, the dialectologists argue that the regularity hypothesis is nothing but a myth. They claim that, in actuality, every word has its own independent history of development.

The fallacy of this argument lies in its underlying assumption or expectation itself. The dialectologists were wrong in expecting that dialect boundaries would be sharply demarcated. After all, the regularity hypothesis does concede the possibility of dialectal borrowings interfering with the effects of a given sound change. If the communities speaking two different dialects have close social contacts in the border areas, they cannot fail to show mutual borrowings. Since borrowings affect lexical items individually, they would have the effect of producing the illusion that each lexical item has a different kind of "spread" concerning a sound change that has affected the dialect. This will clearly explain the haziness or confusion in the phonetic correspondences of items that have been recorded in border areas.

It is also conceivable that a sound change affecting a particular generation would not generally form a sharply demarcating feature between two succeeding generations. Mutual borrowings would exist between two such generations as it exists between two adjacent communities. The general effect of such borrowings would be the normally observed appearance of a change affecting a lexicon gradually. That is, if we examine the records of a language stretching through one or two centuries, we would find that the number of lexical items that show the effects of a given sound change increases gradually from one decade to the next.

For example, it has been claimed that the change of initial *p* to *h* in Kannada has taken about five centuries to completely affect the Kannada lexicon. This claim is based upon the fact that the Kannada inscriptions show fewer words that have been affected by this change in the tenth century as compared to the eleventh or twelfth centuries. The number of such words increases as we proceed up to the fifteenth century. Since borrowing from the speech of persons belonging to the previous generation can be the basis of this fact, it might be a mistake to regard it as indicating the irregular or "gradual" occurrence of the sound change itself.

## 2.4 Exceptions to regularity

In order to appreciate the correctness of the regularity hypothesis, it is therefore necessary to set aside several types of exceptional cases that derive from changes that affect a language *after* a given sound change has taken place in it. As we have seen earlier, such exceptional cases may result primarily from borrowings or grammar-oriented changes. They may also derive, according to some scholars, from certain other factors like onomatopoeia or phonetic symbolism. There may also be other possibilities like the occurrence of free variation in the parent language that may lead to irregular correspondences in the daughter languages.

### 2.4.1 Effects of borrowing

As mentioned earlier, borrowings of lexical items from neighbouring languages or dialects that have not undergone a given sound change can be the cause of some of the exceptions that we observe while studying its effects upon a given language or dialect. The problem, however, is to separate inherited items from such borrowed items. One interesting characteristic of borrowed items that can be helpful in this context is that borrowings generally do not affect basic lexical items. Even among non-basic items, they affect nouns more readily than verbs. Function words such as prepositions or postpositions, auxiliaries or clitics, or inflectional markers like those of tense and aspect are less readily affected by borrowings than other types of words. Even in the case of nouns, specialized words (like technical terms) are more easily borrowed than words that are used in day-to-day life.

If a language shows the effects of a sound change in most of its basic and functional words, but not in many of the non-basic words, we can assume that the exceptions to the sound change occurring in words of the latter type are the results of borrowing. For example, exceptions to the claim that Hindi has changed Sanskrit *š* to *s* are found most commonly in non-basic lexical items, but rarely in basic items.

Many of these exceptions can, therefore, be explained as resulting from the fact that Hindi has borrowed those words from Sanskrit after the sound change had taken place in it. Such borrowings from an earlier stage of a language can occur more readily if that earlier form of the language continues to be used for literary purposes, as has happened in the case of Sanskrit.

(6a) *Sanskrit š changed to Hindi s in basic (inherited) words*

| *Gloss* | *Sanskrit* | *Hindi* |
|---|---|---|
| ten | *daša* | *das* |
| twenty | *vimšati* | *bi:s* |
| cemetery | *šmaša:n* | *masa:n* |
| head | *širas* | *sir* |
| hundred | *šata* | *sau* |
| learning | *šikṣa:* | *si:kh* |
| dried | *šuṣka* | *su:kha:* |

(6b) *Sanskrit š retained as Hindi š in non-basic (borrowed) words*

| | | |
|---|---|---|
| valiant | *šu:ra* | *šu:r* |
| success | *yaša* | *yaš* |
| curse | *ša:pa* | *ša:p* |
| edict | *ša:sana* | *ša:san* |
| destruction | *na:ša* | *na:š* |
| skilful | *kušala* | *kušal* |

Another interesting point is that inherited items would be more numerous in the central part of a given language or dialect area than in its peripheral parts. Hence, if the exceptions of a particular type to a given sound change are more numerous in the peripheral part of a language area rather than in its central part, we can conclude that they are due to borrowing.

For example, Kannada shows a greater number of borrowings from Marathi in Belgaum which is adjacent to the Marathi-speaking area, than in Shimoga which is located in the central part of the language area. Further, the kinds of borrowings that we find in these peripheral areas would also be different as they would depend upon the kinds of languages that are spoken in the adjacent areas. In the above instance of Kannada, for example, there are more borrowings from Telugu than from Marathi in Ballari which is adjacent to a Telugu-speaking area.

When words are borrowed from a language that is very different from the borrowing language in its system of sounds, there would be a need to modify the phonetic structure of borrowed words in order to make them pronounceable. Many of these modifications resemble regular sound changes. Hence, if we are unable to separate such borrowed items from inherited items, they would appear as exceptions to the regularity hypothesis. For example, Prakrit shows one kind of change in words that it has inherited from its earlier stage (Sanskrit) and an entirely different kind of change (or rather modification in the pronunciation) in words that it has borrowed from Sanskrit at a later stage. There are even some doublets like *paṇha* and *pasina* derived from Sanskrit *prašna* 'question'. Notice that in this doublet, the first one manifests the change of medial *šn* to *ṇh*, a change that has regularly affected inherited words (see 31, under 3.3.3), whereas the second one manifests the change of medial *šn* to *sin*, a change that affected borrowed words.

Borrowed words are generally absorbed into a language through modifications of the type mentioned above. They are then treated by the language in exactly the same way in which it treats inherited words. They are kept in a distinct class of their own only when a language has borrowed rather heavily from another language. Sound changes that take place in a language at a later stage would affect borrowed words (that have been absorbed into its system) in exactly the same way in which they affect inherited words. This non-differentiation of inherited and borrowed lexical items by ensuing sound changes makes it even more difficult to differentiate between those two types of words.

### 2.4.2 EFFECTS OF GRAMMAR-ORIENTED CHANGE

Traditionally, grammar-oriented changes of sounds have been termed as analogical changes. The main characteristic of these changes is that they are conditioned by non-phonological factors. They either increase or reduce the scope of morphophonemic alternations that have been introduced by earlier sound changes. Because of this, they generally have the effect of introducing exceptions to earlier sound changes. Traditionally, analogical changes have been considered to be mainly of two types, namely levelling and extension. Levelling reduces the number of morphophonemic alternations that occur in a language or removes them completely, whereas extension increases the scope of an existing morphophonemic alternation.

The change of *u* to *o* that has taken place in Modern Kannada in the case of a small set of verbal bases of the type (c)vc*u* like *koḍu* 'give', described in the previous section (5b), can be regarded as an instance of levelling. Its effect on the grammar of the language is the removal of the morphophonemic alternation occurring between the two sounds in the case of those verbs. It has, however, left the alternation occurring in the case of certain adjectives untouched. By removing the alternation partly from the language, it has made the earlier sound change look irregular. That is, it now appears that the change of *o* to *u* before a high vowel did not affect verbs of the type (c)vc*u*. Actually the verbs did undergo the change earlier, as can be seen from Old Kannada examples, but because of this latter change, they now appear to have been left out by it.

Analogical levelling has taken place rather extensively in the history of Indo-Aryan languages. For example, the verbal roots of Sanskrit show several morphophonemic alternations. In order to account for these alternations and also for the various increments that the verbs take while forming different tense forms, grammarians of Sanskrit had to classify verbs into ten major conjugational classes. Among the middle and modern Indo-Aryan languages, however, most of these alternations have been removed through grammar-oriented changes of different types. For example, the ten classes have been reduced to a single class by analogically extending the first class to cover almost all verbs, and the multiplicity of forms occurring in verbal paradigms has been reduced by extending the stem used in the present tense form to all the other forms.

A comparison of the following forms of the root *pac* 'to cook' occurring in Sanskrit and Pali indicates how this grammar-oriented change has reduced variations occurring in tense forms in Pali (see 7a).

| (7a) | *Gloss* | *Sanskrit* | *Pali* |
|---|---|---|---|
| | he cooks | *pacati* | *pacati* |
| | he will cook | *pakṣyati* | *pacissati* |
| | he cooked | *apakṣi:t* | *apaci* |
| | having cooked | *paktva:* | *pacitva:* |

This analogical extension of the present stem for all the other tense forms in Pali has had the effect of removing several morphophonemic alternations from its tense forms. We can exemplify this by comparing the future forms of Sanskrit and Pali (7b).

| (7b) | *Verbal root* | *Gloss* | *Sanskrit* | *Pali* |
|---|---|---|---|---|
| | *chid* | 'cleaver' | *chetsyati* | *chindissati* |
| | *bhuj* | 'eat' | *bhokṣyati* | *bhunjissati* |
| | *muc* | 'lose' | *mokṣyati* | *muncissati* |
| | *sru* | 'hear' | *sroṣyati* | *sunissati* |
| | *labh* | 'get' | *lapsyate* | *labhissati* |
| | *vas* | 'dwell' | *vatsyati* | *vasissati* |

In addition to these innovative (analogically simplified) forms, Pali also shows forms that are directly derived from the Sanskrit forms given above, such as *checchati* 'he will be clever' or *bhokkhati* 'he will eat', etc. However, later Indo-Aryan languages have lost most of these irregular formations, and have retained only the innovative ones. Thus the result of these grammar-oriented changes is the loss of several morphophonemic alternations that occurred in the earlier stage.

Thus, the basis of grammar-oriented changes (of sounds) is a grammatical paradigm in which one or more morphophonemic alternations occur. We may consider these grammar-oriented changes of sounds as having the following three types of effects upon alternations:

(i) They may reduce the number of alternations by extending one of them at the expense of the rest.

(ii) They may extend the scope of an alternation by bringing in non-alternating forms into its scope.

(iii) They may remove an alternation by converting all alternating items into non-alternating ones.

These grammar-oriented changes are actually changes of grammatical paradigms. They are motivated by the necessity to simplify the paradigms by reducing the complexity that has been introduced into them by earlier sound changes. Notice that all the three types of grammar-oriented changes mentioned above affect alternations in such a way that they ultimately simplify the paradigms in which the alternations occur. Sounds changes, on the other hand, are phonetic in nature, and are motivated by factors that are connected with the articulation of sounds. Their effects upon alternations (see 3.5), may involve the introduction of both simplicity as well as complexity as far as a grammar is concerned. This is because they have no direct motivation in affecting alternations.

Thus, sound changes introduce regularity from the phonetic point of view, but as a result, they may create irregularity in grammatical paradigms. Grammar-oriented (or analogical) changes, on the other hand, remove irregularity from the point of view of paradigms, but as a result, they may introduce irregularity into phonetic correspondences. Sound changes are motivated by the nature of sounds whereas grammar-oriented changes are motivated by the nature of alternations. The effect of the former on alternations is unmotivated (it is only an effect), whereas the effect of the latter on sounds is unmotivated.

We can separate the effects of grammar-oriented change from those of sound change with the help of the distinction in their basic sphere of operation. Grammar-oriented changes can cause alternations inside a morphological paradigm only, whereas sound changes have no respect whatsoever for such paradigms. They affect words that occur both inside as well as outside paradigms. That is, their conditioning is purely phonetic. It is only when a paradigmatic class coincides with a phonological class—as for example, when all the words ending in *u* happen to be verbs of the type (c)vc*u* in a language that underwent a reversal of an earlier change of *o* to *u* before *u* as in Kannada—that separating the effects of the above two types of change becomes rather difficult.

In addition to this motivation of removing complexity from the phonological representation of words and word forms, grammar-oriented changes can have another motivation, which can, in some cases, conflict with the above one. This second motivation derives from the fact that word forms need to be maximally different in order to express the relevant meaning distinctions. This second motivation can induce a grammar-oriented change that increases rather than reduces complexity in the phonological representation of words and word forms. As an example of this tendency, we may perhaps consider the extension of a given morphophonemic alternation to stems and affixes that did not participate in the alternation earlier.

### 2.4.3 ONOMATOPOEIA AND PHONETIC SYMBOLISM

Borrowing and grammar-oriented change help the linguist in accounting for much of the irregularity that one notices while examining the effects of sound change upon the sounds of a given language. There would still be some exceptional cases that remain. According to some scholars, some of these can be accounted for on the basis of the claim that certain marginal types of words that involve factors like onomatopoeia and phonetic symbolism remain outside the sphere of sound changes.

Hörman (1970) defines onomatopoeia as the direct imitation of sounds produced by a resonant object. He distinguishes it from phonetic symbolism by the fact that the latter is the imitation of a quality that the sound as well as the object has in common. Thus, imitation of the tearing sound of a cloth as *parakkane* and of the boiling sound of water as *katakatane* in Kannada is onomatopoeic. On the other hand, the symbolization of bigger objects with a back vowel and of smaller objects with a front vowel, as seen, for example, in pairs of Hindi words, is phonetic symbolism (see 8).

(8)

| Hindi | Gloss | Hindi | Gloss |
|---|---|---|---|
| *lakṛi:* | 'log of wood' | *lakṛa:* | 'a big log of wood' |
| *ghaṛi:* | 'watch' | *ghaṛa:* | 'a big watch' |
| *go:li:* | 'bullet' | *go:la:* | 'bombshell' |
| *paha:ṛi:* | 'hill' | *paha:ṛ* | 'mountain' |

There is probably little evidence to argue that phonetic symbolism resists sound change. Some of the corollaries that derive from it can be shown to be baseless. Hörman (1970) points out, for example, that systematic sampling of dictionaries did not confirm the expectation that terms for larger objects contain *a* sounds rather than *i* sounds.

The case of onomatopoeia, on the other hand, is rather different. Words that show this characteristic generally constitute a separate class by themselves. They imitate actual sounds or sound complexes that occur in nature. Hence, the occurrence of phonetic detail in them is highly motivated. We can, therefore, expect changes that substantially alter the similarity between the imitation and the imitated to be consciously disallowed by language-acquiring individuals. However, it is possible to claim that such words do not form part of the lexicon as such, but stand outside it.

In Kannada, for example, onomatopoeic words occur in very restricted structures and have certain constraints. They appear to have only consonant initials, and involve either reduplication (as in *miramirane* 'shining' or *gaḍagaḍane* 'shaking') or gemination (as in *doppane* 'sound of falling' or *baggane* 'way of catching fire'). The change of initial *p* to *h* does not appear to have affected them, as can be seen in the use of imitative words like *paḷapaḷane* 'way of shining' or *pakkane* 'suddenly'. In fact, there does not appear to be any imitative word that begins with *h*.

### 2.4.4 HYPERCORRECTION

Exceptions to sound change can also be introduced by hypercorrections that occur after a given sound change has taken place. They generally result from the efforts of speakers to borrow pronunciation from dialects or languages that are considered to be prestigious. For example, the

Kannada dialects of several communities in Mysore have undergone the loss of initial *h*. This sound change, however, has not occurred in Standard Kannada. Since Standard Kannada is regarded as the prestigious dialect, especially by the educated class, efforts are made to re-introduce that sound. However, an initial *h* is introduced not only in the case of words that contained the initial consonant earlier (or in the current standard dialect) but also in the case of others that contained only an initial vowel (see 8 of 1.1 for examples). This has led to hypercorrection. Notice that the effect of such hypercorrected usage is the introduction of irregularity into sets of correspondences.

Another instance of hypercorrection is the occurrence of aspirated consonants in Kannada. Originally, the language did not possess aspirated stops, but as a result of borrowings from Indo-Aryan languages, especially from Sanskrit, several words containing these sounds entered into the language. Speakers who are unable to differentiate between words that contained these sounds from words that did not contain them in the lending language use aspiration indiscriminately in both these types of words. They also tend to introduce aspiration into some of the native Kannada words. We can regard this as a case of hypercorrection. Hypercorrection can also introduce irregularity into different sets of correspondences that we establish for native words.

### 2.4.5 SPORADIC CHANGE

Another interesting factor that is considered to be an exception to the regularity hypothesis is the occurrence of sporadic sound changes. These affect individual lexical items rather than a set of such items. That is, sporadic changes are word changes rather than sound changes (see 4 of 1.1). They are considered to differ from regular sound changes on a number of additional aspects such as the following (see Osgood and Sebeok 1965: 148).

(i) Sporadic changes are generally of the type that can as well be termed as speech lapses.

(ii) They are quite frequently affected by sounds at a distance.

(iii) Dissimilation is as frequent as assimilation.

(iv) Metathesis and the dropping of syllables is quite common.

(v) Their field is mostly restricted to a few consonants such as liquids, nasals, or sibilants.

(vi) They typically occur at the time in which a community is using a language rather than the time in which a generation is acquiring it.

Claim (vi) is based upon a study of sound changes and sporadic changes that have taken place in Tulu. A survey of the Tulu-speaking area (Bhat 1970a) has indicated that the two varieties of changes have different types of distribution in that area. While sporadic changes divided the area into two distinct geographical divisions, northern and southern, sound changes divided it into both geographical and social divisions. They helped us not only to differentiate between four geographical divisions—north-east, north-west, south-east and south-west—but also allowed us to establish several social divisions in each area, which were mainly based upon cast distinctions.

This difference in the distribution of sound changes and sporadic changes can be accounted for on the basis of the assumption that sound changes take place when children are acquiring their first language, whereas sporadic changes take place when the language is being used by adult speakers. In the rigid caste system of the Tulu communities, children of different castes would have little contact with one another when they are acquiring their language, and this accounts for the fact that dialectal divisions that are based upon the effects of sound changes is caste-based. On the other hand, adults belonging to different castes have greater opportunity to communicate with one another, and therefore, sporadic changes that take place while adults utilize their language have only geographical constraints.

These differences between sound changes and sporadic changes make it clear that sporadic changes are explanations to some of the apparent exceptions to sound change. In fact, they strengthen the regularity hypothesis by accounting for a few more cases of irregularity that occur in the sets of correspondences that represent a given sound change.

### 2.4.6 FREE VARIATION

Language comparison has brought into light yet another aspect of change that needs explanation before the regularity hypothesis can be accepted. It concerns the occurrence of irregular correspondences. For example, the voicing of initial stops is extremely irregular in Dravidian languages. First, the languages do not agree in showing the initial voicing in that each has a different set of words with voiced initial stops (see 9a). Second, even in the same language, words show alternations between voiced and voiceless stops. For example, a verb may have a voiced initial whereas a derived noun may have the corresponding voiceless initial, or vice versa (see 9b). Dravidianists consider this to be a secondary and irregular development for which no satisfactory explanation has been offered.

(9a) *Variation between two languages*:

| *Gloss* | *Kannada* | *Telugu* |
|---|---|---|
| wheel | *ga:li* | *kalu* |
| ass | *katte* | *ga:ḍida* |
| chink | *kanḍi* | *ganḍi* |
| saw | *garagasa* | *karagasamu* |

(9b) *Variation in the same language (Kannada)*:

| *Voiced initials* | *Gloss* | *Voiceless initials* | *Gloss* |
|---|---|---|---|
| *kaḍe* | 'end' | *gaḍi* | 'limit' |
| *kaṭṭu* | 'tie' | *gaṭṭe* | 'bundle' |
| *kavi* | 'cover' | *gavasaṇige* | 'wrapper' |
| *kampu* | 'fragrance' | *gampu* | 'bad smell' |
| *kattu* | 'neck' | *ganṭalu* | 'throat' |

We can explain the existence of such irregular correspondences by postulating a protostage in which the voiced and voiceless stops were varying freely in the initial position. Such a variation can, at a later stage, lead to arbitrary stabilization of the shapes of forms occurring independently in each daughter language. Thus, if the shape of a nominal form was stabilized with a voiced initial in one language, it could so happen that the same lexical item was stabilized with a voiceless initial in another language. Such an assumption can explain the occurrence of irregular correspondences, without contradicting the regularity hypothesis at the same time.

This possibility of free variations giving rise, at later stages, to irregular stabilizations resulting in the occurrence of irregular correspondences makes it necessary to assume that sound changes are not carried out through intermediate stages of freely alternating forms, as has been hypothesized by some linguists. If we do not make this assumption, we would not be able to differentiate between situations of the above-mentioned type, on the one hand, and situations in which sound changes have given rise to correspondences that are mostly free of any exceptions, on the other. Variations observed in the case of regular sound changes are to be explained as resulting from dialectal borrowings in the geographical, social and temporal levels.

## 2.5 Gradualness hypothesis

Another hypothesis regarding sound change that has led to a lot deal of speculation and discussion in diachronic linguistics is the so-called "gradualness hypothesis". Linguists differ rather widely regarding the exact connotation that they assign to the term "gradualness". It has also been used rather indiscriminately to indicate at least four different aspects of sound change.

### 2.5.1 phonetic gradualness

Some linguists consider the gradualness of sound change to be phonetic. They expect it to affect sounds only in several small, imperceptible steps. For example, they would assume the change of *e* to *i* in a language to have taken place through a number of discrete steps, each represented by a slight rise in tongue-height, the whole process taking decades or may be even centuries to attain completion.

The main basis of this contention is the remarkable regularity of sound changes. It has been argued that the changes could not be so regular if they were not unnoticeable. This argument is based upon the contention that if the changes were noticeable, they would be affected by non-phonetic interferences such as those of meaning, grammatical function, and so on. However, as we have seen earlier, such interferences do not influence sound changes for an entirely different reason. Sound changes occur unconsciously as a generation of speakers is acquiring its first language. The speakers may fail to acquire a distinction in the pronunciation of sounds, or may acquire a new or different distinction. Even if noticeable, neither the speakers nor the adults can do anything about it because what one notices is only the effect of sound change.

On the other hand, scholars who disagree with the above claim regarding phonetic gradualness consider it to be invalid for a different reason. They point out that there are a number of sound changes in the case of which it would be articulatorily impossible to assume any sort of gradualness. Metathesis (*sm* to *mh* in Prakrit), or the change of *q* to *p* or *r* to *l*, are changes of this type, but they are as regular as other sound changes. If these types of changes can occur suddenly (and hence noticeably) and still retain their regularity, there is no reason why the remaining types of sound changes also cannot occur in a similar manner.

Attempts have been made to justify the assumption of phonetic gradualness through dialectal comparisons, or through comparisons of written records of different periods of time. For example, if four different dialects A, B, C and D of a language show a correspondence between *t*, *c*, *š* and *s*, respectively, it could be claimed, according to this assumption, that they represent four different stages of a single change, namely from *t* to *s*. That is, it can be regarded as representing a change of *t* > *c* > *š* > *s* which shows phonetic gradualness. However, such an assumption has to be based upon the gradualness hypothesis itself, and hence it cannot also be regarded as justifying that hypothesis. The use of written records belonging to different periods of time is fallacious for a similar reason and also for the reason that the application of a straight-line succession hypothesis in such cases is not trustworthy (see 1.2).

It is interesting that a dialectal correspondence similar to the one mentioned above occurs in Tulu, but it appears to contradict the contention of phonetic gradualness. The correspondence that occurs in Tulu is between the initial consonants *t*, *c*, *s*, *h* and zero (i.e. complete loss of the initial consonant) as can be seen in the following sets of words:

| (10) | *Gloss* | *Sapaliga* | *Holeya* | *Setti* | *Jain 1* | *Jain 2* |
|---|---|---|---|---|---|---|
| Set I: | | | | | | |
| | wear off | *tare* | *care* | *sare* | *hare* | *are* |
| | sprinkle | *tali* | *caḷi* | *sali* | *hali* | *ali* |
| | bran | *tavḍu* | *cavḍu* | *savḍu* | *havḍu* | *avḍu* |
| | appear | *to:ji* | *co:ji* | *so:ji* | *ho:ji* | *o:ji* |
| | eat | *tini* | *cini* | *sini* | *(tini)* | *ini* |
| | river | *tudɛ* | *cudɛ* | *sudɛ* | *hudɛ* | *(sudɛ)* |
| | stream | *to:ḍu* | *co:ḍu* | *so:ḍu* | *(ho:ḍu)* | *o:ḍu* |
| Set II: | | | | | | |
| | conceiving (of cattle) | *tanɛ* | *canɛ* | *sanɛ* | *hanɛ* | *anɛ* |
| | leaf | *tappu* | *cappu* | *sappu* | *happu* | *appu* |
| | die | *tay* | *cay* | *say* | *hay* | *ay* |
| | cucumber | *tavtɛ* | *cavtɛ* | *savtɛ* | *havtɛ* | *avtɛ* |
| | wear | *tuttu* | *cuttu* | *suttu* | *huttu* | *uttu* |
| | carry on head | *tumbu* | *cimbu* | *sumbu* | *humbu* | *umbu* |
| | see | *tu:* | *cu:* | *su:* | *hu:* | *u:* |

The two Jain dialects, Jain 1 and Jain 2, belong to the northern and southern parts of the Tulu area, respectively. They show some exceptional correspondences resulting apparently from dialectal borrowing. These are given inside brackets. Sapaliga belongs to the northern coastal area, whereas Holeya and Setti belong to the southern coastal area.

According to the phonetic gradualness hypothesis, we may have to claim that the change involved here is *t* > *c* > *s* > *h* > *zero*. The situation, however, is rather complex. The first set goes back to Proto-Dravidian **t* and the second set to **c*. There has been a merger of these two consonants. This, however, did not take place in the Brahmin dialect. There are two possible ways in which we can derive these correspondences through a gradual change of the above type:

(i) The two sounds *t and *c could have merged to *t in a proto-stage, and later on could have changed to other sounds in these dialects.

(ii) The sounds could have merged to *c in a proto-stage, and later on could have changed to these other sounds.

If we choose the first alternative, we will have to claim that in the case of Holeya, Proto-Dravidian *c first changed to *t and then back to *c*. If, on the other hand, we choose the second alternative, we will have to concede that in the case of Sapaliga, Proto-Dravidian *t first changed to *c and then back to *t*. Both these alternatives are clearly unacceptable. We are, therefore, left with an alternative that does not help the hypothesis of phonetic gradualness, namely to assume that the merger itself was to *t* in Sapaliga and to *c* in Holeya.

Another interesting case of gradual phonetic change is considered to be observable in the history of Indo-Aryan languages. The loss of single intervocalic stops in the Modern Indo-Aryan languages is considered to have taken place through several intervening stages—(i) voicing, (ii) spirantization, (iii) reduction to weakly articulated *y* or *v*, and (iv) complete loss. Evidence for each of these stages is considered to be available in the records of Middle Indo-Aryan languages.

### 2.5.2 LEXICAL GRADUALNESS

Another meaning that has been assigned to the term "gradual", as it is applied to sound changes, concerns the lexical aspect. That is, sound changes are said to affect one or two lexical items only to begin with and then to gradually influence the remaining items as well. A further extension of this view is the environmental gradualness according to which a change is said to start as a sporadic event, developing into a conditioned one and then an unconditioned one. According to some scholars, this may further lead to a whole series of sound changes.

The evidence that is considered to support the above assumption is the fact that in a given language area one would notice lesser and lesser number of lexical items that are affected by a given sound change as one moves from the central to the peripheral areas. Similarly, when one examines written texts belonging to different periods of time, one often finds lexical items that are affected by a given sound change increasing gradually to a period in which almost all the words show the effects of that change. However, both these situations can be explained as resulting from borrowings that interfere with the effects of sound change. In the former case, borrowing would be from neighbouring dialects that have not undergone the change, whereas in the latter case or written records it would be from the earlier stage of the language.

As mentioned earlier, languages are affected by "sporadic" changes which occur only in one or two words. It would be a mistake, however, to regard these as representing earlier stages of a sound change in view of the fact that the two appear to derive from distinct mechanisms of change. Sporadic changes have language utilization as their basis whereas sound changes have language acquisition as their basis. There are several characteristic differences between the two (see 2.4.5 and also 1.1), and hence they cannot be regarded as two stages of a single type of change.

### 2.5.3 INDIVIDUAL GRADUALNESS

Another claim that is connected with the notion of gradualness is based upon distinctions that occur among individual speakers of a language who have carried out a given sound change. According to some scholars, a given sound change would be introduced into the language by one or two individuals to start with. It would then be gradually borrowed by more and more individuals as they come into contact, either directly or indirectly, with the innovating individuals. As a result of this borrowing of innovations from one individual to another, sound changes are assumed to spread out like a wave in the social, temporal and geographical spheres. However, this assumption of individualistic gradualness is also based upon evidence that is similar to the one used by the proponents of lexical gradualness. It is based upon variations that occur among individuals in a dialect area in the social, temporal and geographical spheres.

We have already seen how variations occurring in the effects of sound change on lexical items can be accounted for on the basis of cross-dialectal borrowings. Similar explanations can be put forward in the case of variations observed in the speech of individuals belonging to different age groups of a given community as well. If the utilization of lexical items that are affected by a sound change appears to be increasing gradually as one proceeds from higher to lower age groups, it can be argued that the change has actually occurred in the speech of the lower age groups only. We can then regard the forms that show the effects of the change, occurring in the higher age groups, as resulting from the borrowing of lexical items from individuals of lower age groups after the change has taken place. We can also regard the forms that do not show the effects of the change, occurring in the lower age groups, as resulting from borrowings from individuals of higher age groups.

Thus the assumption of individual gradualness for sound change is yet to be properly authenticated. It is most probably the extension of the observation made regarding the gradual spread of lexical innovations or borrowings from one individual to another. Since sound change is considered to be a distinct mechanism, basically different from that of lexical innovation or borrowing, such an extension of the characteristics lexical innovation or borrowing to sound change need not necessarily hold good.

### 2.5.4 ADDITIONAL DERIVED ASSUMPTIONS

Despite its unreliability, gradualness assumption has given rise to a number of additional observations regarding sound changes, which are in the nature of folkloristic tradition, greatly resembling the various theories of language origin, such as the *puh puh* theory, *ding dong* theory or the *bow bow* theory.

Some claim that a sound change would become less and less conspicuous away from the center of change, and that there would be a gradual lessening of its influence rather than any abrupt ending. According to others, the movement of the change, would be most rapid through a territory speaking a single language or closely related languages, and slowest while passing to unrelated languages. There are also claims regarding its spread from one social class to another. Some consider the individuals of an upper class to be the innovators, with the change spreading to lower classes, while others consider the individuals of lower classes to be the innovators. Changes are also considered to cross one another as they move across a given territory, giving rise to the occurrence of different types of effects on language.

It is evident that most of these observations are based upon the assumption that sound changes start with a small set of individuals from whom it is then borrowed by individuals who come into contact with them. There is no evidence that conclusively establishes the latter half of this assumption, except that the effects of sound changes have definite social, temporal and geographical boundaries. The crucial question to be answered here is the following: Are such boundaries caused by the stoppage of the "spread" of a sound change at those particular points? Alternatively, is it possible for the boundaries to result from the fact that the tendency to carry out the relevant sound change arose only among the individuals who were inside those boundaries (with the change taking place simultaneously in the whole area as they acquired the language)? It is not possible to answer this question with our present knowledge of sound changes and hence the assumption of spread for sound changes has no basis as yet.

## 2.6 Direction of Sound Change

While describing or classifying different types of sound changes, we generally make use of pairs of opposing terms such as assimilation and dissimilation, elision and addition, monophonization and diaphonization, split and merger, and so on. The use of such opposing terms can be rather misleading because it creates the impression that sound changes can be bi-directional. That is, the terms appear to indicate that sound changes may occur in either of the two possible directions like removing a sound from a word or inserting one into it, making two sounds similar or dissimilar to one another, combining two sounds into one or splitting one into two, and so on. This impression, however, is a mistaken one.

A closer examination of the actual sound changes that get classified under these opposing terms indicates that they generally involve different types of environments. For example, a mid vowel is raised and turned into a high vowel in Kannada (see 24 of Chapter 3) when followed by a high vowel, whereas a high vowel is lowered to a mid vowel in Telugu (see 22 of Chapter 3) when followed by a low vowel. This latter change has also occurred in Kannada. A front vowel was changed into a back vowel in Tulu (see 16 of Chapter 3), or in Sanketi Tamil (see 23 of Chapter 3) when preceded by a bilabial sound. It was actually a case of rounding followed by backing. On the other hand, a back vowel was fronted (and also made unrounded) in Sinhalese when followed by a high front vowel or semivowel. Thus we have instances here that indicate changes of vowels in all the four directions, namely raising, lowering, backing and fronting (in addition to rounding and unrounding), but the environments which cause these opposing vowel changes are different.

An aspirated stop became an unaspirated one in Sanskrit when it was preceded by another aspirated stop. A similar change occurred in Manipuri when the preceding (rather than the following) syllable had an aspirated stop. Notice, however, that in both these cases the aspirate that caused de-aspiration was non-immediate. It may occur either in the same syllable or in the next syllable but there would always be an intervening vowel. When two aspirated stops occur immediately after one another, they do not show dissimilatory changes of this type. Instead, they tend to become a long (or geminated) aspirated stop.

Statements that have been made regarding nasal + stop clusters can also be misleading for a similar reason. Such clusters are said to assimilate regressively into a double stop in some languages, and progressively into a double nasal in others. But a careful examination of the actual instances that manifest these changes indicates that a double stop occurs when the stop is voiceless, tense, or stressed, whereas a double nasal occurs when it is voiced, lax, or when there is a nasal prosody. Such studies appear to indicate that sound changes, on the whole, are unidirectional. We can generally predict the type of change that can affect a given sound by taking into consideration (i) the nature of the sound that changes, and (ii) the type of environment in which the change occurs. It would not be possible, however, to predict *when* a change is going to take place, or even *whether* a change is going to take place, in a given language. That is, the prediction is about the type of sound changes that might occur in a given type of environment.

### 2.6.1 SOME GENERAL TENDENCIES OF SOUND CHANGE

Cross-linguistic studies have made it possible to establish certain generalizations regarding the way in which sounds tend to change in specific environments. For example, consonants influence the vowels that precede them, especially in the same syllable, in various ways. Apical sounds, including trills, tend to raise the preceding vowels, whereas velars and laterals tend to lower them. This tendency apparently derives from the articulatory distinction that occurs between these two types of consonants. Notice that the production of apical sounds, including trills, involves the raising of the front part of the tongue, whereas the production of velars and laterals involves its lowering.

Flaps can be of two types: retroflexed and non-retroflexed. A retroflexed flap has the property of changing a preceding segment into a retroflex sound. A non-retroflexed flap may also show a similar property, but it would affect the following rather than the preceding segment. This interesting distinction is apparently due to the fact that a retroflexed flap needs to end non-retroflexed, whereas a non-retroflexed flap can end retroflexed.

Labial consonants can make the following vowels rounded and can further change front vowels into back vowels. Palatal consonants, on the other hand, have the effect of raising the following vowel. This is particularly true of the palatal semivowel. Nasals also have the effect of raising the neighbouring vowel.

Stressed vowels and also vowels occurring in closed syllables tend to be lower, whereas unstressed vowels and vowels occurring in open syllables tend to be higher. Nasalization also has a lowering effect upon vowels. On the other hand, vowel length has the effect of making high vowels higher, low vowels lower, front vowels more front and back vowels more back. As against this tendency, shortness has the effect of making vowels get centralized.

Just as consonants can influence neighbouring vowels, vowels can also influence neighbouring consonants. The most common change of this type is the voicing of obstruents when they occur medially between vowels. Such a change may continue further, with the voiced stop becoming a continuant, and getting completely deleted. As against this effect of the intervocal position, word-final position tends to make obstruents devoiced, and get deleted later.

Unstressed front vowels (especially the semivowel *y*) are very effective in palatalizing apical sounds whereas stressed front vowels are effective in palatalizing velar sounds. The former is more prominently raising rather than fronting. Back vowels are more effective than front vowels in inducing fricatives to become retroflex. In fact, front vowels may induce retroflex sounds to become non-retroflex.

There is apparently a need to gather together the effects of various known sound changes in order to establish additional tendencies of change of the above type. It can be supported by the study of distributional limitations of sounds and also of morphophonemic alternations that are reported in descriptive studies of individual languages.

### 2.6.2 MARKED AND UNMARKED SOUNDS

Linguists have found it convenient to sort sounds into pairs in which one member would be considered as marked (i.e. as having a positive feature) and the other member as unmarked. This pairing would be based upon the phonetic properties of sounds. In each pair, the sound that is less complex, more frequent, and acquired earlier by children is considered to be the unmarked sound.

For example, between oral and nasalized vowels, the oral vowel is unmarked and the nasalized one is marked. A voiced stop is a marked sound, whereas the corresponding voiceless stop is an unmarked sound. Voicing is thus a marked or positive feature as long as it occurs with stops. While occurring with vowels, on the other hand, it functions as an unmarked feature. That is, voiced vowels function as unmarked sounds when compared with voiceless vowels. Thus, one will have to make a detailed examination of the various pairs of sounds from different points of view such as their articulation, acquisition, loss through aphasia, frequency of occurrence, and so on, before one can definitely fix their status in the dual classification for markedness.

As for the value of this classification for an understanding of the effects of sound change on language, Greenberg (1966) makes the following postulations:

(i) In the case of isolative changes, the tendency is for the marked sounds to lose their mark.

(ii) In the case of combinatory changes, however, a sound may assimilate to its neighbouring sound, and thereby acquire a mark.

(iii) In cases of complex or conditioned merger, the marked sounds generally lose their mark.

## 2.7 Sound change as rule change

Some linguists have claimed it possible to describe sound changes as rule changes. Their contention is that the internalized knowledge of grammar, occurring in the form of a set of rules, may undergo different types of changes, such as simplification, reordering, loss, etc. of those rules. Sound changes, according to them, can be considered as the results of those changes. That is, they wish to reverse the conception of sound change. Instead of regarding sound changes as changes of sounds that affect grammar in various ways, they wish to claim that sound changes derive from grammar changes. They wish to discard, in effect, the distinction between pronunciation changes (sound changes) and grammar-oriented changes that has been put forth by earlier linguists.

Efforts were made to redraft some of the well-known sound changes as rule changes. For example, the change of word-final *d* to *t* that has occurred in Sanskrit (see 4 of 2.3.1) can be rewritten as resulting from the addition of the following rule to the grammar of Sanskrit at an earlier stage:

(11)

$$\begin{matrix} +\text{ stop} \\ +\text{ voice} \end{matrix} \; > \; -\text{ voice} \; / \; \text{--} \; \#$$

The problem with such rewritings, however, is that grammars

would require rules like (11) only in the case of changes that have given rise to morphophonemic alternations. There could be sound changes like the loss of *s*-*š* distinction that has occurred in Prakrit (see 3 of 2.3.1) which would involve no addition or change of grammar rules as such. In order to account for such changes, it became necessary to have the rules added to the very end of a rule system and then to have them discarded by the next generation of speakers after restructuring the lexicon. This has made the whole enterprise rather cumbersome.

Even in the case of changes that introduce morphophonemic alternations, like the change of *d* to *t* in Sanskrit, there would be lexical items that get affected by the change but still do not participate in the alternation. For example, indeclinable words that ended in *d* earlier would now end in *t*, but being indeclinables, they would not take any suffixes as such, and hence, there would not be any form in which their final *d* could remain unchanged. The occurrence of such words indicates clearly that rule changes are actually the effects of sound change and not the other way round.

It is, therefore, generally conceded that only grammar-oriented changes can be viewed or described as rule changes. Sound changes need to be regarded as distinct from these, and have to be viewed as pronunciation changes. They can only be phonetically conditioned and hence the Regularity Hypothesis that has been put forth by Neogrammarians remains vindicated.

## 2.8 Summary

I have described in this chapter some of the important characteristics of sound change. Regularity (i.e., having only phonetic conditioning) and irreversibility are the two crucial ones among them. Criticisms levelled against these derive primarily from the failure to properly differentiate between sound changes and other changes of sounds. Borrowings of words from neighbouring dialects or languages, grammar-oriented changes of sounds, sporadic changes of sounds, hypercorrection and phonetic symbolism are some of these other types of changes that disturb the effects of sound change on sounds, and thereby make sound changes look irregular. The effects of these additional changes on sounds should be separated from those of sound changes before we can obtain a correct understanding of sound changes.

I have also examined certain additional characteristics that have been ascribed to sound changes, but these are yet to be properly substantiated. For example, the claim that sound changes are gradual involves different types of gradualness, but none of these appears to have been satisfactorily defended. On the other hand, the claim that sound changes are unidirectional appears to be justifiable, but it is yet to be properly substantiated. I have also pointed out that sound changes need to be differentiated from rule changes. The latter are only the effects of sound changes. They cannot, therefore, replace sound changes. We may, however, describe grammar-oriented changes as rule changes.

## FURTHER READINGS

1. Regarding the mechanism of sound change, see
   Hockett 1950. *Age-grading and linguistic continuity and 1965. Sound change.*
   Haugen 1950. *The analysis of linguistic borrowing* (for a characterization of borrowing).
   Jakobson 1941. *Child language, aphasia and phonological universals* (for the parallels between sound change and language acquisition).
   Bhat 1970. *A new hypothesis on language change* (for the distinction between sound change and sporadic change).
2. Regarding the regularity hypothesis, see
   Hock 1986. *Principles of historical linguistics*, ch. 3.
   Bloomfield 1933. *Language*, ch. 20.
   Hockett 1965. *Sound change.*
   Labov 1987. *Resolving the neogrammarian controversy.*
3. Regarding the criticisms of the regularity hypothesis, see
   Labov 1963. *Social motivation of a sound change.*
   Bloomfield 1935. *Language.*
   Malkeil 1962. *Weak phonetic change, spontaneous sound shift and lexical contamination.*
   Hoenigswald 1960. *Language change and linguistic reconstruction.*
4. Regarding the gradualness hypothesis, see
   Bhat 1968. *Is sound change gradual?*
   Chen and Wang 1975. *Sound change: actuation and implementation.*
   Jensen 1983. *Sound change in perception and production.*

5. Regarding the direction of sound change, see
   Greenberg 1966. *Synchronic and diachronic universals in phonology.*

6. Regarding the claim that sound change is rule change, see
   Postal 1968. *Aspects of phonological theory*, ch. 10 and 11.
   Hock 1986. *Principles of historical linguistics*, ch. 11.
   King 1969. *Historical linguistics and generative grammar.*
   Kiparsky 1968. *Linguistic universals and linguistic change.*

# 3

# EFFECTS OF SOUND CHANGE

## 3.1 Introduction

As pointed out in the first chapter, we cannot directly perceive the occurrence of sound changes in a language. They occur at the unconscious level as a generation of speakers is acquiring its first language. However, we can learn about their occurrence from the effects that they leave behind on the pronunciation of words and sentences. It is therefore necessary to examine the various ways in which sound changes can influence various aspects of sounds. We can then establish procedures for reconstructing the sound changes that have taken place in a given language or sets (families) of languages.

In this chapter, we will examine the effects of sound change upon sounds under five different categories.

(i) *Chronological relationship*: We can compare the sound that undergoes a change with the one that results from that change. That is, we can study the effects of sound change from the point of view of the relationship between a sound and its substitute. The difference between the two can be quantitative or qualitative.

(ii) *Syntagmatic relationship*: We can study the manner in which the relationship between a sound and its neighbouring sounds can be affected by a given sound change. It can be assimilation, dissimilation or metathesis.

(iii) *Paradigmatic relationship*: We can study the manner in which the relationship between a sound and the remaining sounds of the language can be affected by a given sound change. There can be a partial or complete merger of two existing sounds, allophonic reassignment of a sound or the split of a sound into two or more distinct sounds.

(iv) *Morphophonemic alternations*: We can study the way in which the morphophonemic alternations that occur in a language can be affected by sound changes. In addition to modifying (or even deleting) the existing alternations, sound changes can also introduce new alternations into a language.

(v) *Contrasts*: We can examine the effects of sound change on the sets of contrasts that occur in a language. A sound change may obliterate them, or shift them from one phonetic distinction to another.

## 3.2 CHRONOLOGICAL RELATIONSHIP

Quantitatively, the relationship between a sound and its substitute can be any of the following:

(i) One to zero as in elision,
(ii) Zero to one as in addition,
(iii) Two to one as in monophonization,
(iv) One to two as in diaphonization, and
(v) One to one or no change as in phonetic shift.

It is also possible to regard the last one as involving a qualitative (rather than a quantitative) relationship between a sound and its substitute.

### 3.2.1 ELISION AND ADDITION

The literature dealing with elision and addition is somewhat unsystematic. This is mainly because scholars have tried to include in this sub-classification a number of factors that are connected with the above two types of change, without analyzing any one of them exhaustively. The terminology used is also rather haphazard. The reason, apparently, is that terms have been coined as and when changes came to the noticc of scholars working on specific languages. They were not meant for an exhaustive representation of the possible types of change. Further, there appears to be a general feeling among many linguists that these relationships derive mainly from sporadic changes rather than from regular sound changes. There is no justification, however, for this latter assumption, as can be seen from the following illustrations.

One interesting criterion that is frequently used in the sub-classification of elision and addition is the place of occurrence of the sound that gets elided or added. The following terminology can adequately represent that factor:

| *Place of occurrence* | *Elision* | *Addition* |
|---|---|---|
| word-initial | procope | prothesis |
| word-medial | syncope | epenthesis |
| word-final | apocope | epithesis |

Word-initial elision is generally termed apheresis, but procope is apparently a more fitting term. Word-final addition is termed excrescence and paragoge also, in addition to epithesis. The above six changes can be illustrated as follows:

(i) *Procope*: This change involves the loss of a word-initial sound. A good example for procope is the loss of initial *h* in the Mysore dialect of Kannada (see 1).

| (1) | *Gloss* | *Standard Kannada* | *Mysore Kannada* |
|---|---|---|---|
| | bird | *hakki* | *akki* |
| | milk | *ha:lu* | *a:lu* |
| | madness | *huccu* | *uccu* |
| | coward | *he:ḍi* | *e:ḍi* |
| | flower | *ha:lu* | *a:lu* |
| | tiger | *huli* | *uli* |
| | village | *haḷḷi* | *aḷḷi* |
| | tile | *hañcu* | *añcu* |

Another example for procope is the loss of initial short vowel in the Sapaliga dialect of Tulu (see 2). This change has taken place when (i) the following consonant was single, (ii) was other than velar or labial, (iii) the following vowel was short, and (iv) a cluster of at least two consonants followed that vowel. Retroflex consonants become non-retroflex in the Sapaliga dialect when they are made initial by this change.

| (2) | *Gloss* | *Shivalli Tulu* | *Sapaliga Tulu* |
|---|---|---|---|
| | throw | *aḍakkɨ* | *dakkɨ* |
| | plough | *aḍappu* | *dappu* |
| | measure | *aḷappu* | *lappu* |
| | weak | *aḷabbɛ* | *labbɛ* |
| | tender | *eḷattɨ* | *lattɨ* |
| | pasture | *oḷaccilɨ* | *laccilɨ* |
| | stumble | *eḍankɨ* | *dankɨ* |
| | crab | *eḍeñji* | *deñji* |
| | left | *eḍattɨ* | *dattɨ* |

(ii) *Syncope*: This change involves the loss of a word-medial sound. It can be exemplified with the help of the change of trisyllabic words into disyllabic ones through the elision of the second vowel, which has taken place in the Mysore dialect of Kannada.

| (3) | *Gloss* | *Standard Kannada* | *Mysore Kannada* |
|---|---|---|---|
| | horse | *kudure* | *kudre* |
| | arecanut | *aḍike* | *aḍke* |
| | door | *ba:gilu* | *ba:glu* |
| | mustard | *sa:sive* | *sa:sve* |
| | inside | *oḷage* | *oḷge* |
| | shop | *angaḍi* | *angḍi* |

Another example for syncope can be the loss of intervocalic stops that has taken place in Prakrit (see 4).

(4)

| Gloss | Sanskrit | Prakrit |
|---|---|---|
| world | *loka* | *loa* |
| all | *sakala* | *saala* |
| affection | *anura:ga* | *aṇura:a* |
| pair | *yugala* | *juala* |
| city | *nagara* | *ṇaara* |
| meal | *bhojana* | *bhoaṇa* |
| heart | *hṛdaya* | *hiaa* |
| separation | *viyoga* | *vioa* |

(iii) *Apocope*: This change involves the loss of a word-final sound. It can be exemplified with the help of the following change of Pali, in which a word-final *t* has been deleted.

(5)

| Gloss | Sanskrit | Pali |
|---|---|---|
| assembly | *pariṣat* | *parisa:* |
| merit (abl.) | *dharma:t* | *dhamma:* |
| that is | *artha:t* | *attha:* |
| wise | *matimant* | *matima:* |
| venerable | *bhagavant* | *bhagava:* |
| from afar | *a:raka:t* | *a:raka:* |
| became | *abhavat* | *ahuva:* |
| having friends | *mitravant* | *mittava:* |

The loss of a sound is frequently accompanied by compensatory changes in the environment. For example, when one of the consonants of a cluster is deleted, we frequently find the following vowel being lengthened as in the Hindi examples in (6).

(6)

| Gloss | Prakrit | Hindi |
|---|---|---|
| cooked rice | *bhatta* | *bha:t* |
| seven | *satta* | *sa:t* |
| eight | *aṭṭha* | *a:ṭh* |
| milk | *duddha* | *du:dh* |
| falsi | *juṭṭha* | *ju:ṭh* |

| *Gloss* | *Prakrit* | *Hindi* |
|---|---|---|
| today | *ajja* | *a:j* |
| dried | *sukkha* | *su:kh* |

Notice that this example of Hindi also involves apocope, as the word-final vowel has been deleted in the case of all these words. It also involves syncope, as one of the consonants in the cluster that precedes the vowel has also been deleted.

(iv) *Prothesis*: This change involves the addition of an initial sound to words. An example for this change is the addition of a *w*-glide that occurs before the initial *o* and *o:* in Kannada. This is only an allophonic change in Standard Kannada, but it has become phonemic in its Mysore dialect, because the vowels *o* and *o:* merged with *a* and *a:* respectively when followed by a low or mid vowel (see also 12 in 3.2.2).

| (7) | *Gloss* | *Proto-form* | *Standard Kannada* | *Mysore Kannada* |
|---|---|---|---|---|
| | inside | **oḷage* | *woḷage* | *waḷge* |
| | agree | **oppu* | *woppu* | *wappu* |
| | ear ornament | **o:le* | *wo:le* | *wa:le* |
| | slant | **o:re* | *wo:re* | *wa:re* |

(v) *Epenthesis*: This change involves the addition of a medial sound to words. It can be exemplified with the help of the following change of Pali in which the vowel *i* has been inserted medially after the first consonant of words beginning with *sn*.

| (8) | *Gloss* | *Sanskrit* | *Pali* |
|---|---|---|---|
| | bathing | *sna:na* | *sina:na* |
| | friendship | *sneha* | *sineha* |
| | oily | *snigdha* | *siniddha* |
| | is fond of | *snihyati* | *sinihyati* |
| | grease | *sneha* | *sineha* |

We may regard the gemination of stops occurring in the third syllable of words of (c)vcvcv pattern in the Havyaka dialect of Kannada as involving the addition of a consonant, but it may as well be regarded as merely the lengthening of the consonant, that is, a qualitative change (see 9).

| (9) | *Gloss* | *Kannada* | *Havyaka* |
|---|---|---|---|
| | vow | *harake* | *harakke* |
| | search | *huḍuku* | *huḍukku* |
| | spring | *orate* | *oratte* |
| | conduct | *naḍate* | *naḍatte* |
| | jealousy | *huḷuku* | *huḷukku* |
| | scream | *kirucu* | *kiruccu* |
| | fold | *maḍike* | *maḍikke* |
| | arecanut | *aḍike* | *aḍakke* |

(vi) *Epithesis*: This change involves the addition of a final sound to words. It can be illustrated with the help of the following instance of Kannada in which the vowel *u* has been added to all words ending in a consonant (see 10).

| (10) | *Gloss* | *Tamil* | *Kannada* |
|---|---|---|---|
| | he | *avan* | *avanu* |
| | she | *avaḷ* | *avaḷu* |
| | they | *avar* | *avaru* |
| | leg | *ka:l* | *ka:lu* |
| | reach | *ce:r* | *se:ru* |
| | who | *ya:r* | *ya:ru* |
| | skin | *tukal* | *togalu* |

In the classification of additions and elisions given above, no distinction is made concerning the type of sounds that get added or elided. The literature contains a special term, "anaptyxis" (or its Sanskrit equivalent svarabhakti), that is used for denoting the addition of a vowel in-between the two consonants of a cluster. This is illustrated by the Pali example given above (see 8) for epenthesis. Since epenthesis indicates medial addition of any sound, this change, in which a consonant has been added medially, can also be included under that category.

### 3.2.2 MONOPHONIZATION AND DIAPHONIZATION

Monophonization is the replacement of a sequence of sounds by a single sound, whereas diaphonization is its reverse, namely the replacement of one sound by a sequence of sounds. These two changes can also be considered as elision and addition respectively, but since the relationship between the sounds involved is more complex than in the case of simple elision and addition, these have been classified separately.

(i) *Monophonization*: The change of Sanskrit *ai* to *e* and *au* to *o* in Pali is a good example for this change (see 11). (The resulting vowel is short before a geminated consonant.)

| (11) | *Gloss* | *Sanskrit* | *Pali* |
|---|---|---|---|
| | oil | *taila* | *te:la* |
| | enmity | *vaira* | *ve:ra* |
| | physician | *vaidya* | *vejja* |
| | rocky | *šaila* | *se:la* |
| | oneness | *aikya* | *ekka* |
| | pale | *gaura* | *go:ra* |
| | pearl | *mauktika* | *mottia* |
| | medicine | *auṣadha* | *o:sadha* |
| | silence | *mauna* | *mo:na* |
| | flood | *augha* | *o:gha* |

(ii) *Diaphonization*: The change of initial *o* and *o:* to *wa* and *wa:* and also *e* and *e:* to *ya* and *ya:* respectively when followed by a low or mid vowel in the next syllable in Mysore Kannada can be an example for this change (see 12).

| (12) | *Gloss* | *Standard Kannada* | *Mysore Kannada* |
|---|---|---|---|
| | pestle | *onake* | *wanke* |

| *Gloss* | *Standard Kannada* | *Mysore Kannada* |
|---|---|---|
| to agree | *oppu* | *wappu* |
| wall | *go:ḍe* | *gva:ḍe* |
| garden | *to:ṭa* | *tva:ṭa* |
| buffalo | *emme* | *yamme* |
| wife | *heṇḍati* | *yaḍti* |
| rat snake | *ke:re* | *kya:re* |
| hen | *he:ṭe* | *hya:ṭe* |

### 3.2.3 PHONETIC SHIFT

Changes in which a sound and its substitute show mainly qualitative differences can be included in this class. Linguists have proposed several sub-classifications in order to take care of these changes. The most important one among them is their division into combinatory and isolative. Changes that are induced or caused by any of the neighbouring segments are called combinatory, whereas the ones that are not effected by any of the neighbouring segments are called isolative. The former involves a conditioned shift whereas the latter involves an unconditioned shift.

(a) *Combinatory change (conditioned shift)*: The change of single, intervocal *l* to *ḷ* and of geminate *ll* to *l* in Marathi can be an example for combinatory change (see 13). It involves the conditioned shift of *l* to *ḷ*.

(13a) *Intervocal l of Sanskrit to ḷ in Marathi*

| *Gloss* | *Sanskrit* | *Marathi* |
|---|---|---|
| fruit | *phala* | *phaḷ* |
| time | *ka:la* | *ka:ḷ* |
| root | *mu:la* | *mu:ḷ* |
| garland | *ma:la:* | *ma:ḷ* |
| bottom | *tala* | *taḷ* |

(13b) *Geminated ll of Prakrit to l in Marathi*

| *Gloss* | *Prakrit* | *Marathi* |
|---|---|---|
| oil | *tella* | *tel* |
| weight | *tulla* | *tol* |
| price | *molla* | *mol* |
| cheek | *galla* | *ga:l* |
| furnace | *culli* | *cu:l* |

(b) *Isolative change (unconditioned shift)*: The change of *n* to *ṇ* that has taken place in Prakrit is an instance of isolative or unconditioned shift. It has affected all the instances of *n* that had occurred in the earlier stage of that language.

(14)

| *Gloss* | *Sanskrit* | *Prakrit* |
|---|---|---|
| bath | *sna:na* | *ṇha:ṇa* |
| noon | *madhya:hna* | *majjhaṇṇo* |
| killed | *jagha:na* | *jahaṇa* |
| dances | *nṛtyati* | *ṇaccai* |
| sound | *svana* | *saṇa* |
| empty | *šu:nya* | *suṇṇa* |
| sky | *nabha* | *ṇaha* |
| fallen | *šanna* | *saṇṇa* |

## 3.3 Syntagmatic relationship

There are mainly three different ways in which the relationship between a sound and its neighbouring sound(s) in a stretch of speech can be altered by a sound change.

(i) The sound under consideration may become more similar (or identical) to the neighbouring sound, giving rise to what is called *assimilation*.

(ii) It may become less similar to its neighbour, thereby introducing *dissimilation* into the stretch.

(iii) It may interchange the place of occurrence with its neighbour, and thereby create the effect called *metathesis*.

Of these three types of change, the first one is the most frequent. Details of these three types of changes in the syntagmatic relationship between sounds are given below.

### 3.3.1 ASSIMILATION

This is a change in which a segment is made more similar or identical with its neighbouring segment. One can study this change from the point of view of (a) the direction of assimilation, (b) the extent of assimilation, and (c) the relation of the assimilating sound with its environment. There are different types of changes that occur under each of these three groups, as shown below.

(a) *Direction of assimilation*: The direction in which an assimilation takes place can be (i) progressive, (ii) regressive, (iii) both progressive as well as regressive, or (iv) mutual as shown below.

(i) *Progressive*: If a sound makes the following sound similar to it, the change is called progressive (or preservative) assimilation. An example for this change can be the assimilation of Sanskrit *y* to the preceding consonant in Pali (see 15).

| (15) | *Gloss* | *Sanskrit* | *Pali* |
|---|---|---|---|
| | impossible | *aśakya* | *asakka* |
| | clarified butter | *a:jya* | *ajja* |
| | enjoyable | *ramya* | *ramma* |
| | sleeps | *supyate* | *suppati* |
| | secret | *rahasya* | *rahassa* |
| | man | *manuṣya* | *manussa* |
| | breaks | *truṭyati* | *tuṭṭai* |

Another example is the change of *i* to *u* in Tulu that has taken place after an initial bilabial consonant (see 16).

| (16) | *Gloss* | *Proto form* | *Tulu* |
|---|---|---|---|
| | handle | **piḍi* | *puḍi* |
| | corpse | **piṇa* | *puṇa* |
| | leave | **biḍu* | *buḍu* |

| Gloss | Proto form | Tulu |
|---|---|---|
| crop | **bi̤lɛ* | *bṳlɛ* |
| heap | **miṭṭɛ* | *muṭṭɛ* |
| tender fruit | **miḍi* | *muḍi* |

These changes are considered to be "progressive" in the sense that the characteristic of the first sound (i.e. being a bilabial sound in the Tulu example) proceeds forward and influences the second sound. Some consider this to be "regressive" as it involves the assimilatory change proceeding backwards.

(ii) *Regressive*: If a sound makes the preceding sound similar to it, the change is called regressive (or anticipatory) assimilation. The assimilation of Old Kannada *r* to the following stop provides an example for this change (see 17).

| (17) | Gloss | Old Kannada | Modern Kannada |
|---|---|---|---|
| | eagle | *pardu* | *haddu* |
| | medicine | *mardu* | *maddu* |
| | having been | *irdu* | *iddu* |
| | correct | *tirdu* | *tiddu* |
| | untie | *bircu* | *biccu* |
| | spread | *parbu* | *habbu* |
| | rush in | *nurgu* | *nuggu* |

The change of initial *d* to *j* in the Shivalli dialect of Tulu, occurring before the palatal (front) vowels *i*, *i:* and *e*, can be given as an additional example for regressive assimilation.

| (18) | Gloss | Sapaliga Tulu | Shivalli Tulu |
|---|---|---|---|
| | much | *diñja* | *jiñja* |
| | fill | *diñji* | *jiñji* |
| | crab | *deñji* | *jeñji* |
| | wash | *dekkɨ* | *jekkɨ* |
| | open | *deppu* | *jeppu* |
| | variety of rice | *di:rsa:lɛ* | *ji:rdari* |

Notice that the effect of front vowels proceeds backwards in the case of this Tulu example. It is therefore called regressive. It is also anticipatory in that the pronunciation of the first consonant anticipates the pronunciation of the following vowel.

(iii) *Progressive and regressive*: It is also possible for a sound to get affected by both progressive as well as regressive assimilations, as for example when it becomes similar to both the preceding as well the following sounds. The change of intervocal aspirated stops like *th, dh, kh* and *gh* of Sanskrit to *h* in Prakrit can be an example for this type of change (see 19). These stops have become similar to both the preceding as well as the following sounds (vowels) by losing their obstruent character. However, a case in which a sound has undergone two different assimilations, one progressive and the other regressive, would be more interesting.

| (19) | *Gloss* | *Sanskrit* | *Prakrit* |
|---|---|---|---|
| | now | *atha* | *aha* |
| | pair | *yu:tha* | *ju:ha* |
| | lip | *adhara* | *ahara* |
| | blood | *rudhira* | *ruhira* |
| | girdle | *mekhala:* | *mehala:* |
| | branch | *ša:kha:* | *sa:ha:* |
| | killed | *jagha:na* | *jahaṇa* |
| | light | *laghuka* | *lahua* |

(iv) *Mutual*: If two sounds assimilate to one another in such a way that both of them are affected by a given sound change, it is called mutual assimilation. An example for this change comes from Prakrit. It has changed Sanskrit *t* to *c* and *d* to *j* before *y*. It has also changed Sanskrit *y* to *c* after *t* and to *j* after *d*. That is, the change of these pairs of co-occurring consonants involves mutual assimilation, as can be seen, for example, in the change of *dy* to *jj* (see 20).

| (20) | *Gloss* | *Sanskrit* | *Prakrit* |
|---|---|---|---|
| | much | *atyanta* | *accanta* |
| | dances | *nṛtyati* | *ṇaccai* |

| Gloss | Sanskrit | Prakrit |
|---|---|---|
| truth | *satya* | *sacca* |
| service | *dautya* | *docca* |
| lightning | *vidyut* | *bijji* |
| today | *adya* | *ajja* |
| garden | *udya:na* | *ujja:na* |
| breaks | *chidyate* | *chijjai* |

(b) *Extent of assimilation*: Assimilation can be complete or partial as shown below.

(i) *Complete*: If an assimilatory change causes two sounds to become identical, it is called complete assimilation. An example for this type of change is Sanskrit *p* becoming *t* before *t* in Prakrit (see 21).

(21)

| Gloss | Sanskrit | Prakrit |
|---|---|---|
| seven | *sapta* | *satta* |
| slept | *supta* | *sutta* |
| secret | *gupta* | *gutta* |
| devotion | *bhakti* | *bhatti* |
| blood | *rakta* | *ratta* |
| eaten | *bhukta* | *bhutta* |
| proper | *yukta* | *jutta* |

(ii) *Partial*: If, on the other hand, a change causes two different sounds to become more similar (than earlier) to one another, but does not make them identical with one another, it is called partial assimilation. The change of *i* to *e* when followed by the vowel *a* in the next syllable, which has taken place in Telugu, is an example for this change (see 22).

(22)

| Gloss | Proto form | Telugu |
|---|---|---|
| join | **piṇ-a* | *penayu* |
| stay | **nil-a* | *nelayu* |
| struggle | **piṇ-a* | *penagu* |

(c) *Relation with the environment*: The distinction involved here is between immediate and distant assimilations, depending upon whether or not the environment that effects the change occurs in the immediate neighbourhood of the sound under consideration.

(i) *Immediate*: If a sound assimilates to an adjacent sound, it is an immediate assimilation. For example, the Sanketi dialect of Tamil has changed an earlier *i* to *u* while occurring immediately after *p* (see 23).

| (23) | *Gloss* | *Tamil* | *Sanketi* |
|---|---|---|---|
| | catch | *piṭi* | *puḍi* |
| | corpse | *piṇam* | *puṇu* |
| | squeeze | *piẕi* | *puḷi* |

(ii) *Distant*: If, on the other hand, a sound assimilates to a non-adjacent sound, it is called distant assimilation. An example for this assimilation is the change of *e* to *i* in Kannada, which has taken place when that sound was followed by a high vowel in the next syllable (see 24).

| (24) | *Gloss* | *Proto form* | *Kannada* |
|---|---|---|---|
| | ear | **kevi* | *kivi* |
| | clear | **teḷi* | *tiḷi* |
| | white | **beḷi* | *biḷi* |
| | hot | **besi* | *bisi* |
| | front | **ediru* | *idiru* |
| | elder | **heri* | *hiri* |

Notice that the three sub-groups of assimilation intersect one another and hence it is possible to characterize a given assimilatory change simultaneously on the basis of two or all the three factors that are involved in these groupings. For example, the first assimilatory change given above (*k* to *g* after *g* in Prakrit) is not only progressive, but also complete as well as immediate. We can think of other similar combinations of these factors, and thereby establish additional varieties of assimilation.

Assimilatory changes that affect vowels have received special attention, as two distinct terms, umlaut and vowel harmony, have been used for describing them. Umlaut can involve the raising, lowering, fronting or backing of vowels, all resulting from the influence of neighbouring vowels. The following alternation of Bengali, resulting from the raising effect of a following vowel, illustrates one type of umlaut:

| (25) | *Root* | *Gloss* | *Third present* | *Third past* |
|---|---|---|---|---|
| | *kɔr* | 'do' | *kɔre* | *korle* |
| | *bɔl* | 'say' | *bɔle* | *bolle* |
| | *rɔ* | 'remain' | *rɔe* | *roille* |
| | *šɔ* | 'suffer' | *šɔe* | *šoile* |
| | *hɔ* | 'be' | *hɔe* | *hole* |

The Telugu example given earlier in (22), on the other hand, exemplifies a lowering umlaut.

In the example for umlaut given in (25), the language still retains the environment that has induced the change. It is also possible to have a situation in which the environment has changed, or the distinction occurring in the environment lost, after it has induced an assimilatory change. In the history of Gulbarga Kannada, for example, the high vowel *i* had contrasted with the mid vowel *e* in that the former had affected the vowel *a* occurring before it and had changed it to *ə*, whereas the latter did not. However, the two had later on merged together to *i* (in certain contexts) and hence the environment for this umlaut is not at the moment available (see 26).

| (26) | *Gloss* | *Standard Kannada* | *Gulbarga Kannada* |
|---|---|---|---|
| | knife | *katti* | *kətti* |
| | ass | *katte* | *katti* |
| | young one | *mari* | *məri* |
| | forget | *mare* | *mari* |

| *Gloss* | *Standard Kannada* | *Gulbarga Kannada* |
|---|---|---|
| cooking | *aḍige* | *əḍgi* |
| arecanut | *aḍake* | *aḍki* |

The term vowel harmony is also used for referring to the assimilatory effects of vowels on neighbouring vowels, but it is not used in cases like the one given above in which the environment that causes the assimilation is missing. Further, the term generally represents morphophonemic alternations that are automatic or affect all the vowels that occur in a particular position. That is, we generally use this term for referring to structural tendencies rather than merely the effects of certain isolated assimilatory changes.

An example for vowel harmony can be the following one from Boro (see 27). In this language, there are two prefixes, *pV* and *sV*, both meaning 'transitive', and a third one, namely *gV*, which is used for deriving adjectives from verbal roots. All these three prefixes change their vowel depending upon the vowel of the following syllable.

| | *Boro* | *Gloss* | *Boro* | *Gloss* |
|---|---|---|---|---|
| (27a) | *diŋ* | 'to whirl' | *pidiŋ* | 'to wind' |
| | *der* | 'to become big' | *peder* | 'to make big' |
| | *mən* | 'to be cooked' | *pəmən* | 'to cook' |
| | *ham* | 'to be good' | *paham* | 'to repair' |
| | *zó* | 'to sit' | *pozó* | 'to seat' |
| | *dúŋ* | 'to be hot' | *pudúŋ* | 'to heat' |
| (27b) | *gi* | 'to fear' | *sigi* | 'to threaten' |
| | *maw* | 'to swing (intr.)' | *samaw* | 'to swing (tr.)' |
| | *goŋ* | 'to bend itself' | *sogoŋ* | 'to bend' |
| | *káw* | 'to be cut' | *sakáw* | 'to cut' |
| | *gó* | 'to slip out' | *sogó* | 'to make to slip' |
| | *búŋ* | 'to be thick' | *subúŋ* | 'to make thick' |
| (27c) | *si* | 'to become wet' | *gisi* | 'wet' |
| | *dér* | 'to be big' | *gedér* | 'big' |

| *Boro* | *Gloss* | *Boro* | *Gloss* |
|---|---|---|---|
| *mən* | 'to ripen' | *gəmən* | 'ripe' |
| *rán* | 'to be dry' | *garán* | 'dry' |
| *zo* | 'to tear' | *gozo* | 'torn' |
| *dúŋ* | 'to be hot' | *gudúŋ* | 'hot' |

### 3.3.2 DISSIMILATION

Even though dissimilation is the reverse of assimilation, only the first and the last of the three sub-classes described above can be employed in this case. The reason for the absence of the second sub-class (complete-partial) in the case of dissimilation is very evident. Some argue, however, that the loss of a sound (i.e. elision, see 3.2.1) constitutes complete dissimilation, and hence other types of dissimilations can be regarded as partial. The following changes belong to the other two sub-divisions of dissimilation.

(a) *Direction of dissimilation*: As in the case of assimilation, dissimilation can also be progressive, regressive or mutual.

(i) *Progressive*: This is a change in which a sound forces a following sound to become dissimilar to it. That is, the effect of a sound is seen on a following sound. An instance of this change has taken place in Manipuri. Aspirated stops, occurring in certain suffixes in this language, have become unaspirated when preceded by roots beginning with an aspirated stop (see 28).

| (28) | *Gloss* | *Proto form* | *Manipuri* |
|---|---|---|---|
| | drink off | **thək-thok* | *thək-tok* |
| | sprinkle out | **khik-thok* | *khik-tok* |
| | begin to stop | **khək-khət* | *khək-kət* |
| | begin to boil | **phut-khət* | *phut-kət* |

(ii) *Regressive*: In this change, a sound forces a preceding sound to become dissimilar to it. In this case, the effect of a sound is observed in a preceding sound. An instance of this type of dissimilation has taken place in Sanskrit (see 29). When an aspirated stop, occurring at the beginning of a syllable, is followed by another aspirated stop either (a) at the end of the same syllable, or (b) at the beginning of the next syllable, it loses its aspiration.

| (29) | *Sanskrit* | *Gloss* | *Sanskrit* | *Gloss* |
|---|---|---|---|---|
| | *dha:vati* | 'runs' | *dadha:va* | 'ran' |
| | *dhvanati* | 'sounds' | *dadhvanuḥ* | 'sounded' |
| | *bhajate* | 'shares' | *babha:ja* | 'shared' |
| | *bha:ṣate* | 'speaks' | *babha:ṣe* | 'spoke' |
| | *bhramati* | 'wanders' | *babhra:ma* | 'wandered' |
| | *bha:sati* | 'shines' | *babha:se* | 'shone' |

The forms given in the third column involve the reduplication of roots of those given in the first column which have an initial aspirated sound. The aspirated sound occurring in the root forces the first consonant of its reduplicated form that precedes it to lose its aspiration. That is, the change involved here is **dhadha:va* > *dadha:va, *dhadhvanuḥ* > *dadhvanuḥ,* etc.

(iii) *Mutual*: It is possible for a dissimilation to be mutual in the sense that two neighbouring sounds become dissimilar to one another through a change that affects both of them.

(b) *Relation with the environment*: As in the case of assimilation, the relation of a dissimilating sound with its environment can be either immediate or distant as shown below.

(i) *Immediate*: Dissimilation can be immediate if a sound becomes dissimilar to a sound that occurs immediately before or after it. The change of o to *a* and *o:* to *a:* after *m* that has taken place in the Ballari dialect of Kannada is an instance of this nature (see 30).

| (30) | *Gloss* | *Kannada* | *Ballari dialect* |
|---|---|---|---|
| | rabbit | *mola* | *mala* |
| | bud | *mogge* | *magge* |
| | crocodile | *mosaḷe* | *masuḷe* |
| | cloud | *mo:ḍa* | *ma:ḍa* |
| | deceit | *mo:sa* | *ma:sa* |

(ii) *Distant*: If a sound becomes dissimilar to a non-adjacent sound, it would be regarded as undergoing distant dissimilation. The two instances of dissimilation given earlier under the progressive and regressive types are both distant dissimilations. Another example of this change has taken place in Tamil (see 31). The vowel **e* of the proto-language has changed into *i* in this language when it was followed by the vowel *a* in the next syllable in words of the (c)vcv type.

(31)

| Gloss | Proto form | Tamil |
|---|---|---|
| to stumble | **eṭaru* | *iṭaru* |
| left | **eṭai* | *iṭai* |
| finger | **veral* | *viral* |
| to scatter | **cetar* | *citar* |
| sweat | **veyar* | *viyar* |

It is possible to think of dissimilatory changes combining with assimilatory changes, as for example, when a distant dissimilation combines with an immediate assimilation or vice versa. Such a change has taken place in Manipuri. Aspirated stops occurring in certain suffixes of this language have become dissimilar to non-adjacent aspirates by becoming unaspirated. But in addition to this, they have also become similar to adjacent sounds (vowels, nasals and semivowels) by getting voiced, as can be seen in the following forms.

(32)

| Gloss | Proto form | Manipuri |
|---|---|---|
| bend out | **khoy-thok* | *khoy-dok* |
| pierce out | **thin-thok* | *thin-dok* |
| sit carelessly | **phəm-thok* | *phəm-dok* |
| uproot | **phoy-thok* | *phoy-dok* |
| bend up | **khoy-khət* | *khoy-gət* |
| pierce up | **thin-khət* | *thin-gət* |
| fill up | **thən-khət* | *thən-gət* |
| begin to think | **khən-khət* | *khən-gət* |

### 3.3.3 METATHESIS

This is a change in which two neighbouring sounds interchange their places of occurrence. Two distinct varieties of metathesis can be established, depending upon whether the two sounds that are involved in the change are adjacent or non-adjacent. However, the known regular instances of metatheses are only of the adjacent type (i.e. immediate metathesis). A good example for immediate metathesis can be found in Telugu (see 33). The first vowel and the following consonant occurring in words of the (c)vcv type have interchanged their places of occurrence in this language under certain restricted environments.

| (33) | *Gloss* | *Proto form* | *Telugu* |
|---|---|---|---|
| | to cuff | **gurd* | *gruddu* |
| | to dig | **tarv* | *travvu* |
| | to push off | **torac* | *tro:cu* |
| | to rub | **urd* | *ruddu* |
| | to increase | **era* | *re:yu* |

Another example for immediate metathesis can be given from Prakrit (see 34). In this language, there has been an interchange of the places of occurrence between fricatives and nasals. The fricatives have also merged together with *h* in this position, which, however, is a different type of change.

| (34) | *Gloss* | *Sanskrit* | *Prakrit* |
|---|---|---|---|
| | Kashmir | *ka:šmi:ra* | *kamhi:ra* |
| | summer | *gri:ṣma* | *grimha* |
| | surprise | *vismaya* | *vimhaya* |
| | heat | *u:ṣman* | *umha:* |
| | Visnu | *viṣṇu* | *viṇhu* |
| | Krishna | *kṛṣṇa* | *kaṇha* |
| | question | *prašna* | *paṇha* |
| | bath | *sna:na* | *ṇha:ṇa* |

## 3.4 Paradigmatic Relationship

There are mainly four different ways in which the effects of sound change can alter the paradigmatic relation of a sound with other sounds occurring in the same language. They are (i) complete merger, (ii) partial merger, (iii) allophonic reassignment, and (iv) split. We may diagrammatically depict these changes, following Hoenigswald (1960: 76–81) with some modifications, as follows:

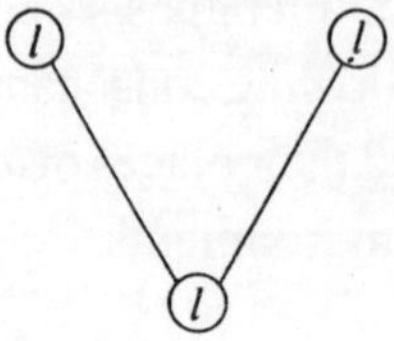


(i) Complete merger

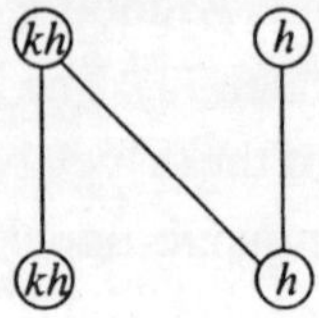


(ii) Partial merger

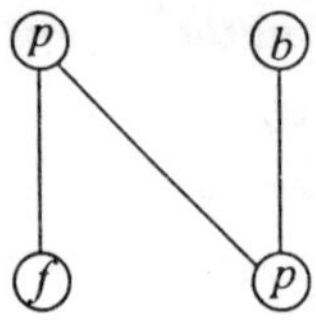


(iii) Allophonic reassignment

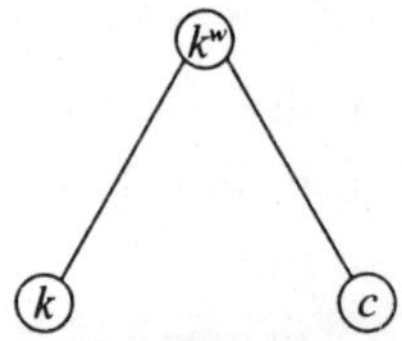


(iv) Split

The four effects of sound change given above on the paradigmatic relationship of sounds can be explained with the help of three distinct processes—(i) merger, (ii) split, and (iii) replacement. Merger affects the relationship directly by nullifying it, whereas split affects it by introducing a new relationship that did not exist earlier. Replacement, on the other hand, affects it by combining with split and thereby changing the characteristics of the relationship. The four kinds of effects mentioned above are as follows:

(i) *Complete merger*: The two laterals *l* and *ḷ* of the proto-language (and occurring as distinct sounds in Shivalli Tulu) have completely merged in the Sapaliga dialect. Notice that in the following examples, both *ḷ* as well as *l* of Shivalli correspond to *l* in Sapaliga.

| (35) | *Gloss* | *Shivalli* | *Sapaliga* |
|---|---|---|---|
| | she | *a:ḷɨ* | *a:lɨ* |
| | sour | *puḷi* | *puli* |
| | rope | *baḷḷɨ* | *ballɨ* |
| | hook | *koḷkɛ* | *kolkɛ* |

| *Gloss* | *Shivalli* | *Sapaliga* |
|---|---|---|
| thread | *nu:li* | *nu:li* |
| tiger | *pili* | *pili* |
| stone | *kalli* | *kalli* |
| spider | *sa:lye* | *ta:lye* |

(ii) *Partial merger*: The sound *kh* of Sanskrit has merged with *h* medially in Prakrit. It has, however, remained unchanged in the initial position.

(36)

| *Gloss* | *Sanskrit* | *Prakrit* |
|---|---|---|
| nail | *nakha* | *naha* |
| face | *mukha* | *muha* |
| hand | *hasta* | *hattha* |
| here | *iha* | *iha* |
| ditch | *kha:ta* | *kha:ya* |
| sword | *khaḍga* | *khagga* |

(iii) *Allophonic reassignment*: An example for this effect is the change of Indo-European **p* to *f* in Germanic languages like English. This change has taken place in all positions except when *p* was preceded by *s*. The sound remained unchanged in this latter position. On the other hand, Indo-European *b*, which did not occur after *s*, changed to *p* in all positions in which it occurred. As a result of this second change, the sound *p*, that occurred after *s* (and remained as *p*) got allophonically reassigned to this latter sound in the Germanic languages.

(37a) *Earlier p changes to f in English*

| *English* | *Other related languages* |
|---|---|
| *father* | Latin: *pater* |
| *fish* | Latin: *piscis* |
| *flow* | Latin: *pluma* |

(37b) *Earlier p remains unchanged after s in English*

| | |
|---|---|
| *spear* | Latin: *sparus* 'dart' |
| *spurn* | Latin: *spernere* |
| *spinach* | Latin: *spina* |

(37c) *Earlier b changes to p in English*

| | |
|---|---|
| *deep* | Lithuanian: *dubùs* |
| *pluck* | Lithuanian: *blužhis* |
| *(s)leep* | Latin: *labi* |

(iv) *Split*: Proto-Indo-European *$k^w$ has split into *k* and *c* in Sanskrit. The distinction between these two sounds was non-contrastive to begin with. It became contrastive when the vowels *o* and *e*, occurring after them respectively, merged with *a*, and the contrast represented by the *e-o* distinction shifted to the *k-c* distinction.

(38)

| *Gloss* | *Sanskrit* | *Latin* |
|---|---|---|
| and | *ca* | *que* |
| five | *pañca* | *quinque* |
| who | *kas* | *qod* |
| horse | *ašva* | *eques* |

If we examine these four paradigmatic effects of sound change from the point of view of the three basic processes given earlier, it could be noticed that partial merger is a combination of merger with split whereas allophonic reassignment is a combination of split with replacement. In the latter case, the change takes place in an environment in which only one of the two sounds under consideration occurred earlier (the position after *s* in the Germanic example given above), and hence it involves no merger as such. (Alternatively, it can take place in all the environments excepting the one in which only one of them occurred.) And as a result of this change, the sound that was occurring in the environment earlier would be replaced by the sound that was not occurring in that environment.

## 3.5 EFFECTS OF SOUND CHANGE ON MORPHOPHONEMIC ALTERNATIONS

A sound change may partly or completely obliterate a morphophonemic alternation. It may alter its nature. It may even introduce new alternations into a language. In order to understand the various effects that a sound change can have upon morphophonemic alternations, it is necessary, first of all, to understand the nature and variety of alternations that can occur in language.

There are mainly four different factors, (as shown below), with reference to which an alternation can be defined.

(i) Automatic vs. non-automatic
(ii) Bilateral vs. unilateral
(iii) Simple vs. complex
(iv) Compulsory vs. non-compulsory

The scope of these factors is not equally extensive, and hence the classification of the alternations obtained through them appears as follows:

- Alternations
  - Automatic
    - Bilateral
      - Compulsory
      - Non-compulsory
    - Unilateral
      - Compulsory
      - Non-compulsory
  - Non-automatic
    - Simple
    - Complex

These distinctions in the morphophonemic alternations of sounds are based upon the occurrence of one or the other of the following types of instances (of word forms) in the environments concerned.

(i) Alternating
(ii) Non-alternating
(iii) Neutral:
  (a) Opposing neutral
  (b) Supporting neutral:
    (1) Determinate supporting
    (2) Indeterminate supporting

### 3.5.1 ASPECTS OF ALTERNATIONS

(a) *Alternating instances*: In order to have a morphophonemic alternation between any two sounds, it is necessary for the two sounds to appear in two different forms of one and the same stem (or affix) occurring in two different environments. For example, the Sanskrit stem meaning 'friend' has two different forms, *suhṛt* and *suhṛd*, of which the former occurs in the nominative (i.e. with no suffix following it) and the latter in the instrumental (i.e. with the suffix *a:* following it). The sound *t* occurs as the final consonant of the stem in the former case and the sound *d* occurs as the final consonant in the latter case. As a result, there is a morphophonemic alternation between the two sounds in the language, namely *t~d*.

The stems or affixes that show such morphophonemic alternations may be termed as *alternating* instances in the environments concerned. [Some scholars define the terms alternating, non-alternating and indeterminate (or neutral) from the point of view of the whole language, rather than from that of certain selected environments. The present stand of defining them only with reference to the environments under consideration has been taken in order to facilitate the use of these concepts for defining the various types of alternations at a later stage.]

(b) *Non-alternating instances*: In contrast to instances that show a given alternation, there can be instances that do not show that alternation. That is, a stem or an affix may occur in both the relevant environments, but still, it may not manifest the relevant alternation. For example, the Sanskrit stem *marut* occurs both in the nominative as well as in the instrumental, but still, it does not show the *t~d* alternation. It has the same form *marut* in both these environments. Such stems or affixes may be termed as *non-alternating* instances in the relevant environments. It is evident that one can talk of non-alternating instances only with reference to alternating instances.

(c) *Neutral instances*: The third possibility is that some stems or affixes may not have any opportunity to place themselves in the environments under consideration because of certain grammatical restrictions. It is also possible that the sounds in question occur in the middle of a stem or an affix and hence, as far as that particular stem or affix is concerned, their occurrence would be restricted to a single environment. For example, Sanskrit has stems like *artha:t* 'that is' and *akasma:t* 'by chance', which are neutral instances for its *t~d* alternation because of they do not occur in the instrumental for grammatical reasons. It also has stems like *šata* 'hundred' and *sva:du* 'sweet', which are neutral instances because the relevant sounds occur only in the non-final position. In both these types of situations we have instances that fail to show the *t~d* alternation.

(c:1) *Opposing and supporting instances*: There can be two different types of neutral instances: (i) those that *oppose* the alternating and non-alternating instances, and (ii) those that *support* them (either jointly or individually). The former (opposing instances) can occur only in the environments in which the alternating and non-alternating instances show identical sounds, or in the environments in which there are no non-alternating instances. Sanskrit does not have any opposing neutral instances in the case of the *t~d* alternation given above because it does not have any word that has *d* in the word-final position.

If we examine the alternation between *r* and *l* that occurs in Manipuri, we can find examples for these various types of neutral instances. The trill *r* alternates with *l* in Manipuri, with the former occurring between two vowels or between a semivowel and a vowel, and the latter occurring initially or after consonants other than the semivowel. We only have alternating instances but not any non-alternating ones. That is, words which allow either of these sounds to occur in both these types of environments invariably show the *r~l* alternation.

| (39) | *Manipuri* | *Gloss* | *Manipuri* | *Gloss* |
|---|---|---|---|---|
| | *ŋa* | 'fish' | *ŋa-rəw* | 'roasted fish' |
| | *ləw* | 'roast' | | |
| | *phi* | 'cloth' | *phi-raŋ* | 'flag' |
| | *laŋ* | 'battle' | | |
| | *ləy* | 'flower' | *ləy-rik* | 'pollen' |
| | *lik* | 'piece' | | |
| | *laŋ* | 'snare' | *təw-raŋ* | 'reed' |
| | *mi* | 'spider' | *mi-raŋ* | 'cobweb' |
| | | | *lik-laŋ* | 'necklace' |
| | | | *səm-laŋ* | 'hair' |

We can, however, have neutral instances that both support as well oppose the alternation. For example, *ŋaprum* 'eel' is an opposing neutral instance as the sound *r* in it occurs after a consonant, whereas *kəplak* 'inside part of knee' is a supporting instance as the sound *l* occurs after a consonant.

(c.1.1) *Determinate and indeterminate instances*: The supporting instances, on the other hand, can occur either (i) in the environment in which the alternating and the non-alternating instances show identical sounds, or (ii) in the environment in which the two have non-identical sounds. It can be regarded as indeterminate in the former case and as determinate in the latter case. For example, words like *akasma:t* 'by chance', given above, are supporting, indeterminate and neutral instances, whereas words like *sada:* 'always' are supporting, determinate and neutral.

The occurrence or non-occurrence of supporting instances does not have any bearing upon the nature of alternations. However, their occurrence is to be specifically noted because such instances (especially the indeterminate ones) are not amenable to reconstruction. They form an interesting limitation to reconstructions that are based upon the nature of alternations.

On the other hand, the occurrence of opposing instances does have a bearing upon the nature of alternations, as can be seen from the classification of alternations suggested below. Such instances, however, are irrelevant as far as the reconstruction of the source of the alternation under consideration is concerned. They are in fact to be derived through diachronic processes (like borrowing or a different sound change) that are unconnected both with the alternation under consideration and the diachronic process that underlies it.

### 3.5.2 CHARACTERISTICS OF ALTERNATIONS

We may describe the characteristics of the various types of alternations given above on the basis of the occurrence or non-occurrence of one or the other of the above-mentioned types of instances in the relevant environments.

(a) *Automatic and non-automatic alternations*: If an alternating set of instances is (i) connected with a single set of non-alternating instances, or (ii) if it has no connection whatsoever with any non-alternating sets of instances, it would represent an automatic alternation.

If, on the other hand, an alternating set of instances is connected with two different sets of non-alternating instances, that is if both the sounds involved in a given alternation occur in sets of non-alternating instances in the relevant environments, it would represent a non-automatic alternation.

The Sanskrit alternation *t~d*, described earlier, occurring in the final/intervocal environments is an automatic alternation. There are, in these environments, (i) a set of alternating instances showing the *t~d* alternation, and also (ii) a single set of non-alternating instances showing a *t~t* relationship, as shown below:

| (40) | Gloss | Nominative | Ablative |
|---|---|---|---|
| (i) *Alternating instances* | | | |
| | wealth | *sampat* | *sampad-a:* |
| | calamity | *vipat* | *vipad-a:* |
| | autumn | *šarat* | *šarad-a:* |
| | friend | *suhṛt* | *suhṛd-a:* |
| (ii) *Non-alternating instances* | | | |
| | being | *sat* | *sat-a:* |
| | wind | *marut* | *marut-a:* |
| | river | *sarit* | *sarit-a:* |
| | good deed | *sukṛt* | *sukṛt-a:* |

English provides a good example for non-automatic alternation. It shows an alternation between word-final *f* and word-medial *v* that is non-automatic. There are instances showing this alternation, but in addition to this, there are also instances that do not show that alternation. The latter have either (i) the sound *f*, both word-initially as well as word-medially or (ii) the sound *v* in both those environments.

(41) *Word-initial* *Word-medial*

(i) *Alternating instances*

| | |
|---|---|
| wife | wives |
| leaf | leaves |
| half | halves |

(ii) *Non-alternating instances with f*

| | |
|---|---|
| cliff | cliffs |

(iii) *Non-alternating instances with v*

| | |
|---|---|
| believe | believes |
| give | gives |
| cave | caves |

(b) *Unilateral and bilateral alternations*: An automatic alternation can be unilateral or bilateral. If the alternating set of instances is not connected with any non-alternating sets of instances, it is a bilateral alternation. If, on the other hand, it co-occurs with another set of non-alternating instances, it is a unilateral alternation.

Havyaka provides an example for bilateral automatic alternation. It shows an alternation in the case of its causative suffix between *s* and *š* with the latter occurring after the palatals *i, i:, y* and *e*, and the former occurring in other environments (see 42). Instances showing this alternation are not connected with any non-alternating instances in these environments and hence it is a bilateral automatic alternation.

(42)

| *After palatals* | | *After other sounds* | |
|---|---|---|---|
| *mi:-šu* | 'to bathe' | *ma: ḍ-su* | 'cause to do' |
| *iḷi-šu* | 'cause to descend' | *koḍu-su* | 'cause to give' |
| *ari-šu* | 'cause to drip' | *to:r-su* | 'cause to see (show)' |
| *bay-šu* | 'cause to scold' | *tar-su* | 'cause to bring' |
| *naḍe-šu* | 'cause to walk' | *uṇ-su* | 'cause to eat' |
| *bare-šu* | 'cause to write' | *horu-su* | 'cause to carry' |
| *be:-šu* | 'to cook' | *ka:su* | 'to heat' |

The automatic alternation between *t* and *d* of Sanskrit given above is unilateral. Notice that there are not only instances like *sampat* 'wealth' that manifest this alternation, but also instances like *marut* 'wind' that do not. In the Havyaka example given above, there are no instances of the latter type that fail to manifest the alternation in the relevant environment.

(c) *Compulsory and non-compulsory automatic alternations*: The automatic alternation (in both its varieties, i.e. bilateral and unilateral) can be further sub-divided into compulsory and non-compulsory. It would be compulsory if the alternating instances *do not* co-occur with opposing neutral instances, whereas if they do co-occur with such instances, it would be non-compulsory.

The unilateral automatic alternation *t~d* of Sanskrit, given above, is compulsory. This is because the consonant *d* does not occur as a word-final consonant in Sanskrit. That is, the alternating instances do not co-occur with opposing neutral instances in the relevant environment.

The Havyaka alternation *s~š* given earlier, which is an example for bilateral automatic alternation, is non-compulsory. This is because there do occur, in Havyaka, instances that have *s* in the palatal environment, such as *hisi* 'to card cotton', *pisuṇṭã* 'naughty boy' and *kesavu* 'a kind of yam'. Since these are opposing neutral instances co-occurring with the alternating instances, the alternation has to be regarded as non-compulsory.

(d) *Simple and complex non-automatic alternations*: A non-automatic alternation can be either simple or complex. It would be simple if it remains unconnected with any other alternation, whereas if it does get connected with some other alternation, it would be complex. The English alternation *f~v*, given in (41), is an example for simple non-automatic alternation. Another example can be the Manipuri alternation *r~l* given in (38).

Sanskrit shows an alternation between a final *k* and an intervocal *j* which is connected with another alternation between a final *ṭ* and an intervocal *j* (see 43). It is complex because the two alternations are interconnected. It is also non-automatic because *k* can occur in non-alternating instances in the relevant environments as seen in the pair of forms, *sarvašak* 'omnipotent' *sarvašaka:*.

(43)

| Gloss | Nominative | Ablative |
|---|---|---|
| physician | *bhiṣak* | *bhiṣaj-a:* |
| priest | *ṛtvik* | *ṛtvij-a:* |
| yoke | *yuk* | *yuj-a:* |
| garland | *srak* | *sraj-a:* |
| king | *ra:ṭ* | *ra:j-a:* |
| worship | *iṭ* | *ij-a:* |
| creation | *sṛṭ* | *sṛj-a:* |

### 3.5.3 EFFECTS OF SOUND CHANGE ON ALTERNATIONS

As has been already pointed out above, sound changes can have any of the following effects upon morphophonemic alternations:

(i) *Obliteration*: A sound change may obliterate an existing morphophonemic alternation either completely or partially.

(ii) *Change*: A sound change may change the nature of an existing alternation in one of several ways.

(iii) *Addition*: A sound change may introduce new alternations into the language, or it may widen the scope of an existing alternation.

(i) *Obliteration of an alternation*: An existing alternation can get obliterated through sound change if all the alternating instances that represent the alternation are changed into non-alternating ones. This can happen if the two alternating sounds in question are made identical (i.e. completely merged together) as a result of a sound change affecting one or both of them.

The obliteration of an alternation may be partial or complete. It would be partial if it has affected an alternation only in some of the environments in which the alternation had occurred in the earlier stage. In such a situation, its effect upon the alternation would be the narrowing of the scope of that alternation. A complete obliteration, on the other hand, would have the effect of removing the alternation from all the environments in which it had occurred earlier.

The merger of Sanskrit *n* and *ṇ* in Hindi had the effect of completely obliterating the *n*~*ṇ* alternation that had occurred earlier in Sanskrit (see 44). For example, such an alternation occurred in the instrumental suffix of Sanskrit. The suffix had the nasal *ṇ* in it when it was preceded by *r, ṛ* or *ṣ* (except when there was an intervening dental or retroflex stop), and the nasal *n* in it in other contexts. Hindi shows only *n* in all contexts.

| (44) | *Gloss* | *Sanskrit* | *Hindi* |
|---|---|---|---|
| | by Rama | *ra:m-eṇa* | *ra:m-ne* |
| | by heat | *ta:p-ena* | *ta:p-ne* |
| | by the enemy | *šatru-ṇa:* | *šatru:-ne* |

### 3.5.4 INTRODUCING NEW ALTERNATIONS INTO A LANGUAGE

A sound change can introduce a new, non-existing alternation into a language by converting a set of non-alternating instances (i.e. stems that had identical forms in two different environments) into alternating ones. For example, in the Kudali dialect of Marathi, the merger of word-final *k* and *g* has given rise to an automatic unilateral alternation between the two sounds as can be seen in the following sets of forms:

| (45a) | *Kudali* | *Gloss* | *Kudali* | *Gloss* |
|---|---|---|---|---|
| | *Dhək* | 'cloud' | *Dhəga* | 'cloud' (oblique form) |
| | *bak* | 'bend' | *bagəy* | 'cause to bend' |
| | *ak* | 'fire' | *agi* | 'fires' |

The alternation is unilateral because of the existence of non-alternating forms of the following type:

| (45b) | *Kudali* | *Gloss* | *Kudali* | *Gloss* |
|---|---|---|---|---|
| | *šik* | 'learn' | *šikay* | 'teach' |
| | *khak* | 'armpit' | *khako* | 'armpits' |
| | *kaḷok* | 'darkness' | *kaḷoka* | 'darkness' (oblique form) |

Another example can be given from Havyaka in which the loss of certain word-final consonants has resulted in the introduction of new alternations into the language (see 46).

| (46) | *Havyaka* | *Gloss* | *Havyaka* | *Gloss* |
|---|---|---|---|---|
| | *avu* | 'they' | *avara* | 'their' |
| | *eŋgo* | 'we' (excl.) | *eŋgaḷa* | 'our' |
| | *avã* | 'he' | *avana* | 'his' |
| | *ava* | 'she' (hon.) | *avaḷa* | 'her' |

## 3.6 EFFECTS OF SOUND CHANGE ON CONTRASTS

A sound change can have one of the following effects on phonemic contrasts:

(i) It may obliterate an existing contrast.

(ii) It may shift the contrast from one set of segments or features to another set, or it may shift it to some other aspect of phonology such as the syllabic structure.

(iii) It may combine these two effects (obliteration and shift) in various ways.

A change may affect a contrast only partially in limited environments, leaving it untouched elsewhere (conditioned change), or it may affect it unconditionally, effecting a shift or obliteration in all the instances in which it occurred.

It must be noted here that sound changes are incapable of introducing new contrasts into a language. Only borrowings and morphological changes have this capacity of introducing new contrasts into the phonological system of a language.

### 3.6.1 OBLITERATION OF CONTRASTS

A contrast between two segments (or between a segment and its absence) can get obliterated due to loss of phonetic differences that occur between them. Such an obliteration is called merger if two segments are involved, and loss if a segment and its absence are involved. Notice, however, that merger and loss need not always lead to the obliteration of contrasts. They may lead to the shift of contrasts as well (see 3.6.2).

The obliteration of contrast can be complete or partial depending upon whether it takes place in all the environments in which the sounds in question contrast, or only in some of the environments.

(a) *Complete obliteration through merger*: The merger of *s* and *š* in Hindi has completely obliterated the contrast that occurred earlier between these two sounds in Sanskrit (see 47).

| (47) | *Gloss* | *Sanskrit* | *Hindi* |
|---|---|---|---|
| | hundred | *šata* | *sɔ* |
| | hear | *šruṇ* | *sun* |
| | ten | *daša* | *das* |
| | seven | *sapta* | *sa:t* |
| | all | *sarva* | *sab* |
| | juice | *rasa* | *ras* |

(b) *Complete obliteration through loss*: Certain dialects of Kannada have completely lost the sound *h*, which has led to the complete obliteration of the contrast between *h* and its absence that existed in Kannada earlier (see 40).

| (48) | *Gloss* | *Standard Kannada* | *Mysore Kannada* |
|---|---|---|---|
| | milk | *ha:lu* | *a:lu* |
| | sour | *huḷi* | *uḷi* |
| | fry | *huri* | *uri* |
| | say | *he:ḷu* | *e:ḷu* |
| | potato | *a:lu* | *a:lu* |
| | chisel | *uḷi* | *uḷi* |
| | blaze | *uri* | *uri* |
| | get up | *e:ḷu* | *e:ḷu* |

(c) *Partial obliteration through merger*: The sounds *k* and *c* have merged together to *c* initially before palatal vowels in Telugu. This partial merger has led to the partial obliteration of the contrast that had existed earlier between *k* and *c* in the proto-language (see 49a).

| (49a) | *Gloss* | *Proto form* | *Telugu* |
|---|---|---|---|
| | cry | **ki:ru* | *ci:ru* |
| | touch | **keṇayu* | *cenayu* |
| | be small | **kiluku* | *cikku* |
| | scratch | **ci:ru* | *ci:ru* |
| | vie with | **ceṇayu* | *cenayu* |
| | be caught | **ciluku* | *cikku* |

The obliteration of the contrast is only partial as it occurred only before palatal vowels. In other positions, the contrast has remained intact as can be seen in the following pairs of words:

| (49b) | *Telugu* | *Gloss* | *Telugu* | *Gloss* |
|---|---|---|---|---|
| | *kanu* | 'to see' | *canu* | 'to go' |
| | *kuṭṭu* | 'to prick' | *cuttu* | 'to wrap' |

(d) *Partial obliteration through loss*: The loss of pre-nasal *k* in English (which, however, is retained in the spelling) has led to the partial obliteration of the contrast between *k* and its absence (see 50). The contrast remains intact in other positions.

| (50) | | |
|---|---|---|
| | knight | night |
| | know | no |
| | knot | not |
| | kill | ill |
| | kin | in |

In Hindi, a two-fold loss has led to the partial obliteration of contrast between two segments (in addition to the partial obliteration of the contrast between these two segments and their absences, respectively). The word-final vowels *a* and *i* that occurred in Middle Indo-Aryan (MIA) were lost in Hindi, and as a result there is no contrast between these two vowels in the word-final position in Hindi.

| (51a) | *Gloss* | *MIA* | *Hindi* |
|---|---|---|---|
| | leaf | *patta* | *pa:t* |
| | lip | *oṭṭha* | *oṭh* |
| | armpit | *kakkha* | *ka:kh* |
| | servant | *da:sa* | *da:s* |
| (51b) | night | *ratti* | *ra:t* |
| | sight | *diṭṭhi* | *di:ṭh* |
| | eye | *akkhi* | *ã:kh* |
| | woman | *na:ri* | *na:r* |

### 3.6.2 SHIFT OF CONTRASTS

Contrast between two segments, or between a segment and its absence, can get shifted to some other set of segments as a result of sound change. This can happen, for example, if the two segments under consideration merge together, and the merger is accompanied by a compensatory change in the neighbouring segments. The contrast would then be automatically shifted to this neighbouring differentiation.

For example, the contrast between voiced aspirates and voiceless unaspirates was partially shifted to the following vowels in Punjabi. This resulted from the following two sound changes. (a) Initial voiced aspirates were devoiced and de-aspirated. This made them identical with the respective voiceless unaspirates in that position. (b) Pitch of the vowels that followed these voiced aspirates was lowered (see 51b). This made the vowels different from the respective vowels that occurred after voiceless unaspirates. This latter distinction was therefore able to represent the set of contrasts that was represented by the former distinction at an earlier stage.

| (51a) | *Gloss* | *Sanskrit* | *Punjabi* |
|---|---|---|---|
| | bitter | *kaṭuka* | *koṛa:* |
| | work | *karma* | *kamm* |
| | wood | *ka:ṣṭha* | *ka:ṭh* |
| | thread | *tantu* | *tand* |
| | oil | *taila* | *tel* |

| | Gloss | Sanskrit | Punjabi |
|---|---|---|---|
| | leaf | *patra* | *patta:* |
| | five | *pañca* | *pañj* |
| | wheel | *cakra* | *cakk* |

| (51b) | *Gloss* | *Sanskrit* | *Punjabi* |
|---|---|---|---|
| | pitcher | *ghaṭa* | *kàṛa:* |
| | horse | *ghoṭaka* | *kòṛa:* |
| | thick | *ghana* | *kàṇa:* |
| | wealth | *dhana* | *tàn* |
| | smoke | *dhu:ma* | *tù:ã* |
| | boiled rice | *bhakta* | *pàtt* |
| | difference | *bheda* | *pèd* |
| | at once | *jaṭiti* | *càṭṭ* |

It is also possible that the neighbouring segments were already different in a non-contrastive way, and the merger of the segments in question has merely brought them into a contrastive opposition. This could be the situation in the Punjabi change given above, as pointed out earlier (see 2.2).

A contrast may also shift to some other aspect of phonology, as a result of a merger caused by sound change. Supposing, for example, that a language had both short and long vowels contrasting only in the initial syllable of words of cvcv type. Supposing, further, that at a later stage, all words of cvcv type with a long vowel in the first syllable lost their final vowel and became monosyllabic (there being no monosyllabic words earlier). In this latter stage there would not be any contrast between short and long vowels. However, the contrast represented by them earlier would not be lost for the language, because it would now be represented by a difference in the syllabic structure of the relevant words.

### 3.6.3 PARTIAL OR COMPLETE SHIFTS

A shift of contrast can be partial or complete. It can be partial in two different senses. Since the merger of two different segments can be partial, occurring only in some environments but not in others, the contrast that they represented earlier would be shifted to some other distinction only in those environments. It would be kept unchanged in other environments. The second possibility is that, even though the merger is complete, an alternative distinction that is to represent the contrasts might be available only in some of the environments in which the merger took place. This second type of partial shift can occur in the case of the first type of partial shift as well.

An example for the second type of partial shift can be given from the Gulbarga dialect of Kannada [see also (26)]. In this dialect, word-final *e* has become *i* and thereby merged with the vowel *i* that already existed in that position. However, the vowel *a* occurring in the preceding syllable shows a distinction, as it became *ə* when followed by an earlier *i* and remained as *a* when followed by an earlier *e* (that changed to *i*). Thus, the contrast carried by the *i-e* distinction was partially shifted to the *ə-a* distinction. The contrast was lost when the former distinction occurred in words in which the preceding syllable had some other vowel (see 52).

| (52) | *Gloss* | *Standard Kannada* | *Gulbarga Kannada* |
|---|---|---|---|
| *Shifting of contrast when the preceding syllable had the vowel a* | | | |
| | knife | *katti* | *kətti* |
| | ass | *katte* | *katti* |
| | young one | *mari* | *məri* |
| | forget | *mare* | *mari* |
| | having tied | *kaṭṭi* | *kəṭṭi* |
| | platform | *kaṭṭe* | *kaṭṭi* |
| *Loss of contrast when the preceding syllable had other vowels* | | | |
| | parrot | *gubbi* | *gubbi* |
| | sleep | *nidde* | *niddi* |
| | fire | *benki* | *binki* |
| | worry | *cinte* | *cinti* |
| | needle | *su:ji* | *su:ji* |
| | owl | *gu:ge* | *gu:gi* |

It must be noted here that a contrast may remain mostly intact even in cases in which a conditioned merger is not followed by a conditioned shift. This is possible in cases where a conditioned merger results in a morphophonemic alternation. For example, the merger of final *t* and *d* in Sanskrit has resulted in a *t~d* alternation as in *šarat~šarada:*, *suhṛt~suhṛda:* etc. (see 3.5.2), and hence the contrast between the two sounds *t* and *d* as seen in pairs of words such as *šarat* and *marut* are retained as the alternation occurs in the former item only and not in the latter item.

Grammar-oriented changes may reintroduce the phonetic distinctions that have been lost by such conditioned changes, but they can do so only in the case of items in which the contrast had been retained with the help of morphophonemic alternations.

### 3.6.4 SYNTAGMATIC AND PARADIGMATIC SHIFTS

The replacement of one or both the contrasting segments by some other segment or segments, without in any way disturbing the contrast that was represented by the former, can also be regarded as a shift of contrast, but this would be a different type of shift. In the previous instances the contrast was shifted from a segment to its neighbouring segment or to some other aspect of phonology, whereas in the present case, it shifts to the segment that replaces the original segment. That is, the former is a syntagmatic shift, whereas the present one is a paradigmatic shift.

An example for this latter type of shift can be given from Sanskrit. The retroflex sibilant *ṣ* of Sanskrit is assumed to have been a palatal sibilant earlier. It was changed into a retroflex one through a sound change. We can consider this change as causing a shift of contrast from an earlier *s-š* distinction to a later *s-ṣ* distinction. Similarly, in the history of English, an earlier dental series (*t̪, n̪*) is said to have given place to an alveolar series, giving rise to shifts of contrasts. For example, the sets of contrasts that were represented by the distinction between dental stops and labial stops earlier are now represented by the distinction between alveolar stops and labial stops.

Paradigmatic shifts can also be partial in that they may take place only in certain restricted environments. In Marathi, for example, the *c-j* contrast of Old Marathi was shifted from palatal affricates (voiced and voiceless) to alveolar ones before non-front vowels, whereas it remained with palatal affricates before front vowels.

## 3.7 Summary

I have described in this chapter five different ways in which the effects of sound change on the sounds of a language can be viewed. The first three of these represent three different ways in which we can view the relationship between the changing sounds and their environment (chronological, syntagmatic and paradigmatic) whereas the last two represent the effects that sound changes can leave behind on the phonological system of languages.

Notice that there are five different ways in which one and the same set of sound changes can be viewed. They provide five different facets of sound change. They are not therefore exclusive of one another. An assimilatory change, for example, may involve the introduction of an alternation into a language. Similarly, the loss of a set of sounds may lead to the loss of a set of contrasts. What is now needed is an exhaustive study of these various effects of sound change from the point of view reconstruction. That is, we have to find out which of these effects can help us to reconstruct the sound change that has produced that effect and which of them cannot.

Chapter 4 indicates the direction in which such an exhaustive study can be carried out.

### Further readings


1. Regarding the effects on chronological, syntagmatic and paradigmatic relationships, see
   Lehmann 1963. *Historical linguistics*, ch. 10,
   Hock 1985. *Principles of historical linguistics*, ch. 5–6.
   Ultan 1971. *A typological view of metathesis.*
2. Regarding the effects on alternations, see
   Bybee 1980. *Morphemic change from inside and outside the paradigm.*
3. Regarding the effects on contrasts, see
   Hoenigswald 1960. *Language change and linguistic reconstruction.*

# 4

# RECONSTRUCTION OF SOUND CHANGE

## 4.1 Methods of reconstruction

This chapter examines the various procedures that can be used for reconstructing individual instances of sound change. There are two reasons why these procedures of reconstruction are needed. First, most of the languages of the world have no written records. Therefore, we can learn about sound changes that have taken place in their earlier stages only with the help of reconstruction procedures.

Second, even in the case of the few languages in which earlier stages have been preserved in the form of inscriptions and literary works, these procedures of reconstruction are needed because, as discussed in the first chapter, written history is not very dependable. It may involve shifts in the dialects that are used for writing, and hence the differences that we notice between records of two different stages may or may not represent changes from an earlier stage to a later stage. It is therefore necessary to check the authenticity of sound changes that we establish on the basis of written records with the help of more reliable reconstruction procedures. Further, reconstruction procedures can complement written history as the latter is generally fragmentary in its preservation of earlier stages.

The procedures that we use for reconstructing sound changes

crucially depend upon the effects that sound changes leave behind on various aspects of language. We can observe these effects either by studying individual languages, or by comparing two or more languages. In the former case, it would be the structure of the phonological system or its relation with the morphological system that provides the basis for reconstruction. In the latter case, on the other hand, reconstruction depends upon the *differences* that we notice between compared languages. That is, if the languages are to be derived from one single proto-language, the *differences* that occur between them have to be explained as resulting from sound changes or other types of language changes that have taken place in one or the other of the compared languages.

We can examine the effects of sound change upon a given language from several different points of view as shown in the previous chapter. Each of them provides a different set of hypotheses regarding the relationship between sound changes and their effects upon language. These hypotheses can then be utilized for formulating different procedures for reconstructing sound changes, or for recovering other aspects of language that have been altered, obliterated, shifted, or even newly created by those changes.

For example, the study of genetically related languages and dialects has made it possible to claim that sound changes are *incapable* of introducing new phonological contrasts (or rather sets of oppositions, see below) into a language. Sound changes can either obliterate an existing contrast, or shift it from one phonetic distinction to another. And as can be seen from the discussion that follows, the reconstruction procedure that is generally termed "comparative method" is mainly based upon this particular hypothesis regarding the effects of sound change upon phonological contrasts.

Similarly, what has been called the method of "internal reconstruction" is mainly based upon the assumption that sounds which alternate morphophonemically in a language are the results of splits that had taken place earlier in the history of that language. Such splits can only result from sound changes. That is, the mere occurrence of a morphophonemic alternation in a language allows us to apply the method of internal reconstruction and go back to an earlier stage of that language in which there was no corresponding alternation.

While applying the above two methods of reconstruction, however, linguists make use of several other procedures of reconstruction of which some are based upon hypotheses that are of questionable validity. The problem here is that linguists desire to reconstruct words and word forms that look like real words. This would not be possible if only the most reliable reconstruction procedures, like the two described above are used. Since the procedures used for reconstruction are not generally listed and evaluated individually, it is rather difficult to evaluate the reconstructions that are obtained through the application of those procedures.

Linguists differentiate between comparative method and the method of internal reconstruction by claiming that comparative method utilizes material extracted from the comparison of two or more languages, whereas internal reconstruction utilizes material extracted from the study of only one single language. Some linguists have suggested a new name, "external reconstruction", for the former, in order to bring out this supposed distinction between these two methods of reconstruction. Notice, however, that such a classification of the methods of reconstruction does not provide us with any basis for evaluating them.

A classification of the methods (or rather the procedures) of reconstruction that is based upon their underlying principles or hypotheses would be more helpful in evaluating or maintaining the validity of our reconstructions. As can be seen from the following description of these two well-known methods of reconstruction, a classification based upon the underlying hypotheses cuts across that well-known classification. Further, the latter generally tends to overlook the hypotheses, which actually provide the basis for evaluating the results of all these reconstructions.

It would therefore be more helpful to postulate a multiplicity of reconstruction procedures, whose number would depend upon the number of hypotheses that have been formulated regarding sound changes—hypotheses that can fruitfully be utilized for formulating procedures of reconstruction. The validity of each one of these procedures can then be regarded as depending directly upon the validity of the respective underlying hypotheses.

### 4.1.1 COMPARATIVE METHOD

The term "comparative method" is generally used for referring to a reconstruction procedure (or rather a set of procedures) by which "cognate" forms of words occurring in different genetically related languages are compared and the ancestral form for each word is reconstructed. Consider, for example, the following four sets of words belonging to two different dialects of Tulu, namely Shivalli and Sapaliga:

| | (1) | *gloss* | *Shivalli* | *Sapaliga* |
|---|---|---|---|---|
| Set I | 1. | tamarind | *puḷi* | *puli* |
| | 2. | thin | *teḷpu* | *telpu* |
| | 3. | she | *a:ḷi* | *a:li* |
| Set II | 4. | worm | *puḷi* | *puri* |
| | 5. | time | *poḷtu* | *portu* |
| | 6. | fowl | *ko:ḷi* | *ko:ri* |
| Set III | 7. | popped rice | *pori* | *pori* |
| | 8. | bamboo ladder | *kerpu* | *kerpu* |
| | 9. | measles | *go:ra* | *go:ra* |
| Set IV | 10. | to stitch | *poli* | *poli* |
| | 11. | to learn | *kalpu* | *kalpu* |
| | 12. | four | *na:li* | *na:li* |

We may compare the words occurring in each of these four sets from the point of view of the sounds *l*, *ḷ* and *r*, and establish correspondences of sounds for the two languages. For example, in the case of all the three words that occur in the first set, Shivalli has the sound *ḷ* in all contexts in which Sapaliga has the sound *l*. That is, there is an *ḷ~l* correspondence in each of the three words given in set I, and hence set I represents a set of correspondences for *ḷ~l*. There are three other sets of correspondences in the remaining three sets of cognate words as shown below:

| | *Shivalli* | *Sapaliga* |
|---|---|---|
| Set I: | *ḷ* | *l* |
| Set II: | *ḷ* | *r* |
| Set III: | *r* | *r* |
| Set IV: | *l* | *l* |

Since all these four sets of correspondences occur in identical environments, we need to reconstruct four different sounds for the proto-language. This claim is based upon the hypothesis that contrasts (or rather sets of oppositions) cannot be newly introduced into a language through sound changes. For example, in the case of the first two sets, Shivalli uses the same sound, namely *ḷ*, but Sapaliga uses different sounds, namely *l* in the first set and *r* in the second set. This latter difference cannot be the result of a sound change because it represents a set of contrasts in Sapaliga. We therefore have to conclude that the two sets of correspondences represent distinct proto-sounds. Sets I and IV and II and III have identical sounds in Sapaliga, but distinct sounds in Shivalli. Hence, we need to reconstruct distinct proto-sounds for all these sets of correspondences.

The general procedure in comparative method is to reconstruct **r* and **l*, respectively, for the third and fourth sets of words on the basis of the fact that the two dialects show the same sound in these forms. The reconstruction would be **ḷ* for the first set on the basis of Shivalli evidence (i.e. in view of the fact that Shivalli differentiates between *l* and *ḷ*). We are to assume that Sapaliga has changed this sound (a retroflex lateral) to *l*. For the second set, there is a need to reconstruct a proto-sound that is different from all the three (**r*, **l* and **ḷ*) that have been reconstructed so far. The nature of this sound, however, can only be determined by obtaining data from other related languages. This is because Shivalli fails to distinguish that sound from *ḷ*, whereas Sapaliga fails to distinguish it from *r*. Languages like Tamil, Malayalam or Old Kannada provide a basis for this reconstruction in that they do possess a sound (a retroflex continuant) for this set, which is different from *l*, *r* and also *ḷ*.

Notice that the hypothesis mentioned above regarding contrasts provides the basis only for claiming that the four sets of cognate words given above represent four different sounds in the proto-language. The exact phonetic make up of the sounds has to be determined on the basis of certain other hypotheses, such as for example, that a sound which is the same in both the compared languages is to be considered to have remained unchanged. This latter hypothesis, however, is not as reliable as the one concerning the loss of contrasts mentioned earlier.

A more complex example for comparative method, involving environmental factors, is the following which makes use of words from Kannada, Tamil and Telugu. Reconstructed forms of the parent language for these cognate words are also given below. Justifications for the suggested reconstructions are provided in the following paragraphs.

| (2) | *Gloss* | *Kannada* | *Tamil* | *Telugu* | *Reconstruction* |
|---|---|---|---|---|---|
| 1. | ear | *kivi* | *cevi* | *cevi* | **kevi* |
| 2. | small | *kiṟu* | *ciṟu* | *ciṟu* | **kiṟu* |
| 3. | scatter | *kedaṟ* | *citaṟ* | *cedaṟu* | **kitaṟ* |
| 4. | leg | *ka:l* | *ka:l* | *ka:lu* | **ka:l* |
| 5. | bear fruit | *ka:y* | *ka:y* | *ka:yu* | **ka:y* |
| 6. | eye | *kaṇ* | *kaṇ* | *kanu* | **kaṇ* |
| 7. | shout, rage | *kele* | *cilai* | *celayu* | **kilai* |
| 8. | pond | *koḷa* | *kuḷam* | *kolanu* | **kuḷam* |
| 9. | join | *ku:ḍu* | *ku:ṭu* | *ku:ḍu* | **ku:ṭu* |
| 10. | verdigris | *kilubu* | *cilumpu* | *cilumu* | **kilumpu* |
| 11. | fort | *ko:ṭe* | *ko:ṭṭai* | *ko:ṭa* | **ko:ṭṭai* |
| 12. | be entangled | *sikku* | *cikku* | *cikku* | **cikku* |
| 13. | to wind | *suttu* | *cuṟṟu* | *cuṭṭu* | **cuṟṟu* |
| 14. | restrain | *seṟe* | *ciṟai* | *ceṟa* | **ceṟai* |
| 15. | reach | *se:r* | *ce:r* | *ce:r* | **ce:r* |

Since these lexical items are considered to be "cognates", that is inherited by these languages from their parent language, we do not have to do anything about the phonetic similarities that occur among these forms. That is, similarities derive from the fact that all these words have come from a single source. We only have to explain the *differences* that occur between them. We do this by postulating changes for one or the other of these languages.

When we compare the forms of cognate 1 'ear', for example, we notice that the forms differ from one another on two points:

(i) The initial consonant is *k* in Kannada and *c* in Tamil and Telugu.

(ii) The first vowel is *i* in Kannada and *e* in Tamil and Telugu.

The second difference is generally explained as resulting from a change that occurred in the history of Kannada language, namely the raising of *e* to *i* before a single consonant, when followed by a high vowel. That is, Tamil and Telugu are considered to maintain the vowel as it was in the parent language, whereas Kannada is considered to have changed it to *i*. Notice that the first two cognates show a contrast between *i* and *e* in the case of both Tamil and Telugu but not in Kannada. This fact forms the basis of this reconstruction.

The first difference given above, on the other hand, is accounted for on the basis of the postulation of a change of *k* to *c* before front vowels in Tamil and Telugu. The reason why we do not consider this *k-c* difference as resulting from a change of *c* to *k* in Kannada is that there are other sets of words for which an earlier *c* needs to be reconstructed. Compare the following sets of words that occur in example (2):

(a) Cognate words 1, 2, 3, 7 and 10 in which *c* of Tamil and Telugu corresponds to *k* of Kannada.

(b) Cognate words 4, 5, 6, 8, 9 and 11 in which *k* of Tamil and Telugu corresponds to *k* of Kannada.

(c) Cognate words 12, 13, 14 and 15 in which *c* of Tamil and Telugu corresponds to *s* of Kannada.

Notice that the first two sets of correspondences are in complementary distribution. The *c~k* set occurs before palatal (front) vowels whereas the *k~k* set occurs before non-palatal vowels. The third set (*c~s*), on the other hand, occurs before both these types of vowels (before palatal vowels in 12, 14 and 15 and before non-palatal vowels in 13). It therefore needs to be differentiated from the other two in our reconstruction.

Further the change of *k* to *c* before front vowels (called "palatalization") would be a "natural" sound change, whereas that of *c* to *k* in the same environment (in case we postulate such a change) would be an unnatural one (see 2.6). We generally prefer to reconstruct proto-forms that require the postulation of natural rather than unnatural sound changes.

Cognate 3 involves the following three additional differences:

(i) The second consonant is voiced (*d*) in Kannada and Telugu and voiceless (*t*) in Tamil.

(ii) The word ends in a consonant in Kannada and Tamil and in a vowel in Telugu.

(iii) The vowel *e* of Kannada and Telugu (in the first syllable) corresponds to the vowel *i* of Tamil.

In order to account for the first difference (numbered iii), we postulate a change of intervocalic voicing of stops for Kannada and Telugu. This would account for similar differences occurring in cognates 9 and 10 as well.

The second difference (numbered iv) results from the addition of the vowel *u* to all consonant-ending words in Telugu. This change accounts for similar differences occurring in cognates 4, 5, 6, 7, 8 and 15.

The third difference (numbered v) results from the neutralization of the distinction between *i* and *e* before a single consonant and the vowel *a* in all these three languages. This neutralized vowel appears as *e* (a mid vowel) in Kannada and Telugu and as *i* (a high vowel) in Tamil. The change is exemplified by cognates 7 and 14 as well. A comparable neutralization of the distinction between *o* and *u* needs to be postulated in order to account for the difference occurring in the first vowel of cognate 8.

The exact value of the vowels that can be postulated for the parent forms of these cognates, in the case of both these neutralizations, however, cannot be determined on the basis of the forms given above. The value of the vowels, given in the reconstructed forms, has been determined on the basis of additional data (i.e. on the basis of forms occurring in languages such as Tulu that have not undergone the change). Forms occurring in one of these languages in which the vowel occurs in a different environment were also helpful in determining the value of those vowels. This latter procedure involves the method of internal reconstruction (see 4.1.2).

Cognate 6 involves neutralization of the *n-ṇ* distinction in Telugu, and cognate 8 involves the corresponding neutralization of the *l-ḷ* distinction in the same language. There is also an irregular change of word-final *m* to *n* in Telugu in the latter case. Cognates 10 and 11 are similar in that they show a cluster reduction (*mp* to *b* or *m* and *tt* to *t*) in Kannada and Telugu. Cognate 11 (and also 14) shows the change of *ai* to *e* in Kannada and to *a* in Telugu. Cognates 12 and 15 show the change of initial **c* to *s* in Kannada, and cognate 13 shows the change of **r̲r̲* to *tt* in Kannada and to *ṭṭ* in Telugu.

### 4.1.2 INTERNAL RECONSTRUCTION

As we have seen in the previous section, comparative method establishes reconstructions on the basis of a comparison of cognate forms extracted from two (or more) related languages. The method of internal reconstruction, on the other hand, does so on the basis of a comparison of cognate forms that are extracted from one single language. That is, words that show a morphophonemic alternation in a given language are reconstructed as having no such alternation in the parent language. The method is mainly based upon the assumption that morphophonemic alternations result from sound changes that affect the relevant sounds conditionally.

As we have seen in the third chapter, morphophonemic alternations can result from sound changes only if they affect roots or affixes that participate in paradigms. It is also necessary for the changes to affect the roots or affixes differently in different parts of the paradigm. Consider the change of *b*, *d* and *g* to *p*, *t* and *k*, respectively, of Boro, which has taken place conditionally, that is only when the sounds were followed by the consonants *p*, *t* or *k*. This change could introduce a set of morphophonemic alternations into the language, namely *b~p, d~d* and *g~k* because of the following reasons:

(i) The language had a set of words that ended in the consonants *b*, *d* or *g*.

(ii) The language also had a set of words and affixes that began with the consonants *p*, *t* or *k*.

(iii) These latter words and suffixes occurred after the words mentioned in (i).

Since the sound change mentioned above (devoicing of *b*, *d* and *g*) affected the words mentioned in (i) only when they were followed by words or affixes that had an initial *p*, *t* or *k* but not otherwise, it was able to introduce a morphophonemic alternation into the language as shown below:

| (3a) | *Boro* | *Gloss* | *Boro* | *Gloss* |
|---|---|---|---|---|
| | *záb* | 'hcap up' | *zap-krú* | 'heap up everything' |
| | | | *zab-ər* | 'rubbish heap' |
| | *gáb* | 'cry' | *gap-kráw* | 'be always crying' |
| | | | *gab-rám* | 'groan' |
| | *ud* | 'camel' | *ut-kəw* | 'camel' (acc.) |
| | | | *ud-nə* | 'camel' (dat.) |
| | *bələd* | 'bull' | *bələt-pər* | 'bulls' (pl.) |
| | | | *bələd-ni* | 'bull's' (gen.) |
| | *zalug* | 'black pepper' | *zaluk-kəw* | 'black pepper' (acc.) |
| | | | *zalug-aw* | 'black pepper' (loc.) |

We can apply the method of internal reconstruction to these sets of alternating forms and claim that in an earlier stage of this language all of them had only one form in the environments concerned. We cannot, however, reconstruct the phonetic make up of those forms. The final consonants occurring in them need to be different from *p*, *t* and *k* respectively in view of the occurrence of the following sets of words. This is in spite of the fact that in Boro, the voiceless stops, *p*, *t* and *k*, do not occur in the word-final position and hence cannot be followed by words or affixes that begin with *p*, *t* or *k* (see 3b).

| (3b) | *Boro* | *Gloss* | *Boro* | *Gloss* |
|---|---|---|---|---|
| | *pando* | 'lotus' | *bandar* | 'granary' |

| *Boro* | *Gloss* | *Boro* | *Gloss* |
|---|---|---|---|
| *para* | 'small village' | *bara* | 'side of a boat' |
| *taw* | 'to be tasty' | *daw* | 'to go ahead' |
| *dikáŋ* | 'to lift' | *digiŋ* | 'direction' |
| *kubəy* | 'to throw' | *gubəy* | 'real' |

Another example for this procedure of internal reconstruction can be the following one of Sanskrit in which words show a *t~d* alternation.

| (4a) *Gloss* | *Nominative Singular* | *Instrumental Singular* | *Instrumental Plural* |
|---|---|---|---|
| Set I: | | | |
| 1. wind | *marut* | *marut-a:* | *marud-bhiḥ* |
| 2. river | *sarit* | *sarit-a:* | *sarid-bhiḥ* |
| 3. world | *jagat* | *jagat-a:* | *jagad-bhiḥ* |
| 4. good deed | *sukṛt* | *sukṛt-a:* | *sukṛd-bhiḥ* |
| 5. lightning | *taḍit* | *taḍit-a:* | *taḍid-bhiḥ* |
| 6. triple string | *trivṛt* | *trivṛt-a:* | *trivṛd-bhiḥ* |
| 7. world conqueror | *višvajit* | *višvajit-a:* | *višvajid-bhiḥ* |
| 8. wing | *garut* | *garut-a:* | *garud-bhiḥ* |
| 9. silkworm | *košakṛt* | *košakṛt-a:* | *košakṛd-bhiḥ* |
| 10. mountain | *kṣma:bhṛt* | *kṣma:bhṛt-a:* | *kṣma:bhṛd-bhiḥ* |
| Set II: | | | |
| 11. autumn | *šarat* | *šarad-a:* | *šarad-bhiḥ* |
| 12. assembly | *pariṣat* | *pariṣad-a:* | *pariṣad-bhiḥ* |
| 13. misfortune | *a:pat* | *a:pad-a:* | *a:pad-bhiḥ* |
| 14. wealth | *sampat* | *sampad-a:* | *sampad-bhiḥ* |
| 15. calamity | *vipat* | *vipad-a:* | *vipad-bhiḥ* |
| 16. hump | *kakut* | *kakud-a:* | *kakud-bhiḥ* |
| 17. sprout | *udbhit* | *udbhid-a:* | *udbhid-bhiḥ* |
| 18. friend | *suhṛt* | *suhṛd-a:* | *suhṛd-bhiḥ* |
| 19. rock | *dṛṣat* | *dṛṣad-a:* | *dṛṣad-bhiḥ* |
| 20. religious writings | *upaniṣat* | *upaniṣad-a:* | *upaniṣad-bhiḥ* |

The Sanskrit words given above have been arranged into two sets of words, 1–10 and 11–20. Both these sets show an alternation between *t* and *d*. The first set has *d* only before a voiced consonant (i.e. in the fourth column), whereas the second set has that consonant in the intervocal position (third column) as well. The two sets contrast in this third column.

By applying the method of internal reconstruction to these words, we are able to claim that the *t~d* alternation, occurring in these words, did not exist in an earlier stage of Sanskrit (which we may call Pre-Sanskrit). That is, we are able to claim that the words must have had a single form each, uniformly, in all these three columns in Pre-Sanskrit. The alternation must have resulted from one or more changes that had taken place in the pre-history of Sanskrit.

We can split the *t~d* alternation shown by these lexical items into two different alternations on the basis of the environments that determine their occurrence. The first one is the alternation occurring between the environments (i) word-final and (ii) intervocal (i.e. between columns two and three). Notice that the words of the first set (1–10) do not show this alternation. They have uniformly the voiceless consonant *t* in both these environments. Only the words of the second set (11–20) show this alternation. The second *t~d* alternation occurs between the environments (i) word-final and (ii) before a voiced consonant. This alternation occurs in both these sets of words.

Let us examine the first alternation to begin with. We may apply the method of internal reconstruction to the second set of words, which does manifest this alternation, and postulate that the words of that set had a single form in both these environments. However, we need to postulate further that they had *d* (and not *t*) as the stem-final consonant, because they contrast with words of the first set which have a stem-final *t* in both the environments mentioned above (i.e. word-final and intervocal). That is, the first *t~d* alternation resulted, according to this reconstruction, through the devoicing of the stem-final consonant *d* of the words of the second set, when no vowel followed it. Notice, however, that the exact phonetic make up of this reconstructed sound (namely that it is *d*) cannot be derived from the procedure mentioned above. We can only claim that it needs to be distinct from *t* because of words occurring in set I.

In the case of the second alternation also, we can apply the method of internal construction and claim that the alternation did not occur at an earlier stage, and that it has resulted from sound change. However, we need to postulate two different sound changes in order to account for its occurrence in the two sets of words as shown below:

In the case of the first set of words, we can claim that Pre-Sanskrit had a final *t* in these words in both these environments. The change of *t* to *d* in the second environment (i.e. *voicing* before a voiced consonant) was responsible for the occurrence of this alternation in those words. In the case of the second set of words, on the other hand, we need to postulate that the words uniformly had a stem-final *d* in Pre-Sanskrit (as claimed earlier). The *t-d* alternation occurring in them resulted from the *devoicing* of that sound when either a voiced consonant or a vowel (which is also voiced) did not occur after it.

Thus the reconstruction of the first set of words for Pre-Sanskrit would be with a stem-final *t* throughout and for the second set of words with a stem-final *d* throughout, as in (4b).

(4b) *Reconstructed Pre-Sanskrit forms*

Set I:

| | | | |
|---|---|---|---|
| 1. wind | **marut* | **marut-a:* | **marut-bhiḥ* |
| 2. river | **sarit* | **sarit-a:* | **sarit-bhiḥ* |
| 3. world | **jagat* | **jagat-a:* | **jagat-bhiḥ* |

etc.

Set II:

| | | | |
|---|---|---|---|
| 11. autumn | **šarad* | **šarad-a:* | **šarad-bhiḥ* |
| 12. assembly | **pariṣad* | **pariṣad-a:* | **pariṣad-bhiḥ* |
| 13. misfortune | **a:pad* | **a:pad-a:* | **a:pad-bhiḥ* |

etc.

Another example for the application of the method of internal reconstruction is the following, which is made up of certain verbal forms of Manipuri, denoting a distinction of directionality (see 5a).

Notice that the alternation occurs in the suffix rather than the verbal base in these forms.

(5a) *c~j~s alternation of Manipuri*:

| | *Manipuri* | *Gloss* | *Manipuri* | *Gloss* |
|---|---|---|---|---|
| Set I: | | | | |
| | 1. *thet* | 'insert' | *thet-cin* | 'insert in' |
| | 2. *sit* | 'sweep' | *sit-cin* | 'sweep in' |
| | 3. *hut* | 'bore' | *hut-cin* | 'bore in' |
| | 4. *phuk* | 'pull' | *phuk-cin* | 'pull in' |
| | 5. *hip* | 'tie' | *hip-cin* | 'tie in' |
| Set II: | | | | |
| | 6. *hi* | 'bend' | *hi-jin* | 'bend in' |
| | 7. *tha* | 'send' | *tha-jin* | 'send in' |
| | 8. *thin* | 'pierce' | *thin-jin* | 'pierce in' |
| | 9. *khoy* | 'bend' | *khoy-jin* | 'bend in' |
| Set III: | | | | |
| | 10. *pi* | 'give' | *pi-sin* | 'give in' |
| | 11. *cət* | 'go' | *cət-sin* | 'go in' |
| | 12. *yok* | 'rear up' | *yok-sin* | 'rear up in' |
| | 13. *tin* | 'gather' | *tin-sin* | 'gather in' |
| | 14. *nəm* | 'darken' | *nəm-sin* | 'darken in' |
| | 15. *pay* | 'fly' | *pay-sin* | 'fly in' |

The forms given above involve the derivation of one of the four directional bases that occur in Manipuri. The suffix meaning 'in' occurring in them shows three different forms, namely *cin*, *jin* and *sin*. The three are in complementary distribution. We need to postulate the following two rules in order to describe this distribution:

(i) *cin* and *jin* occur after verbal bases that have an initial aspirate (*kh*, *th* or *ph*) or an initial fricative (*s* or *h*), and *sin* occurs elsewhere.

(ii) Among the first two forms, *cin* occurs after verbal bases that have a final voiceless sound (*p*, *t* or *k*), and *jin* occurs elsewhere.

These morphophonemic alternations between (i) an affricate and a fricative (*cin* and *jin* vs. *sin*) on the one hand, and between (ii) a voiceless affricate and a voiced affricate (*cin* vs. *jin*) on the other, can be the bases of internal reconstruction. We can claim that in an earlier stage called Pre-Manipuri, this directional suffix with the meaning 'in' had only one form, and as a result of two sound changes, the suffix has split into three different forms. We may reconstruct the suffix as **cin* and postulate the following sound changes:

(i) It became **sin* through fricativization of the initial consonant when not preceded non-immediately by an aspirate or a fricative.

(ii) It became **jin* in other environments (i.e. when not preceded non-immediately by an aspirate or a fricative), but when immediately preceded by a voiced sound. (It remained as *cin* in other contexts.)

Manipuri shows a comparable alternation between *t*, *th* and *d*, and between *k*, *kh* and *g* (involving aspiration and voicing) in the same set of environments in the case of suffixes like *tok* 'out' and *kət* 'up', as seen in the following examples:

(5b) *th~d~t and kh~g~k alternations of Manipuri*:

Set I:

| | | | |
|---|---|---|---|
| *pi-thok* | 'give out' | *pi-khət* | 'give up' |
| *cət-thok* | 'go out' | *cət-khət* | 'go up' |
| *cen-thok* | 'run out' | *cen-khət* | 'run up' |

Set II:

| | | | |
|---|---|---|---|
| *hi-dok* | 'trim out' | *hi-gət* | 'trim up' |
| *thin-dok* | 'pierce out' | *thin-gət* | 'pierce up' |

Set III:

| | | | |
|---|---|---|---|
| *khik-tok* | 'sprinkle out' | *khik-kət* | 'sprinkle up' |
| *hek-tok* | 'pluck out' | *sup-kət* | 'cover up' |

We may use the method of internal reconstruction in these cases also and reconstruct the suffixes as having a single form each (**thok* 'out' and **khət* 'up') in Pre-Manipuri. We may assume further that the Manipuri forms given above have derived from them through (i) de-aspiration (and spirantization in the case of **c*) when preceded, non-immediately, by an aspirate or a fricative, and (ii) voicing when immediately preceded by a voiced sound, and further, when the earlier change (de-aspiration) has taken place.

There is an interesting point that needs to be noted here. When we claim that all the morphophonemic alternations that occur in a given language can be regarded as derivable from earlier sound changes, we do not imply that there could be a proto-stage in which the language did not contain any morphophonemic alternations whatsoever. Such a claim would go against the generally known fact (i.e. a language universal) that no known language is devoid of any morphophonemic alternations. However, alternations frequently get deleted due to following sound changes, and also due to grammar-oriented changes. Hence even if we get rid of all the existing alternations of a language while reconstructing its proto-form, there would still be others that have been lost by the language before it attained its present form.

### 4.1.3 MULTIPLICITY OF THE BASES OF RECONSTRUCTION

The above two methods of reconstruction actually use several different procedures, each based upon a distinct assumption or hypothesis. These hypotheses differ rather markedly from one another in their reliability, and because of this, the two reconstruction methods (that make use of procedures that are based upon these hypotheses), have a complex set of reliability values.

For example, both comparative method as well as the method of internal reconstruction make use of a procedure by which a lost contrast, or rather a lost set of oppositions, is recovered. This procedure is based upon the hypothesis that a set of oppositions cannot be newly introduced into a language (see 4.3.1). This reconstruction procedure is highly reliable and hence reconstructions based upon it are of indisputable validity. However, in both comparative method as well as internal reconstruction, it does not show up as a distinct procedure. Instead, it gets mixed up with several other procedures, such as those based upon the naturalness of a postulated change (e.g. change of *k* to *c* before front vowels is more natural than *c* to *k* in the same environment), occurrence of contrast versus complementation, economy or path of least resistance, etc. These latter procedures are clearly less reliable as compared to the former procedure.

In order to properly evaluate the reconstructions that we establish on the basis of comparative method or internal reconstruction, it is therefore necessary to specify the exact procedures that we use, and the principles or hypotheses that form the basis of those procedures. We can then evaluate the procedures individually on the basis of an evaluation of their underlying hypothesis and can therefore have a better understanding of the validity of the reconstructions that we obtain through the application of these methods.

## 4.2 Nature of the sound–meaning relationship

It is very well known that the sounds of a language do not by themselves convey any meaning (except in certain special instances of phonetic symbolism and onomatopoeia). Sounds are in fact used to form sequences called "morphemes", and these sequences in their turn are used to convey meaning. This interesting property of language, namely that of connecting sounds with meaning through an intermediate level of morphemes, is called "double articulation".

The relationship between sounds and meanings, formed through this intermediate level of morphemes, is purely arbitrary. That is, one cannot generally give any reason why a particular meaning should be conveyed by a particular sequence of sounds in one language, and by an entirely different sequence of sounds in another language. Consider, for example, the object that English indicates by the sequence *tree*. Kannada uses a different sequence, namely *mara* for this purpose and Sanskrit uses a still different sequence, namely *vṛkṣa*. There is no natural connection between any of these sequences of sounds and the object that they denote in any of these languages. It is simply a convention that has been handed down from generation to generation in the history of these languages that determines the relation between these sequences of sounds and the objects or meanings that they represent.

These relationships are also independent of one another in the sense that the use of a particular sequence of sounds to convey a particular meaning in a given language is not conditioned by the use of any other sequence in the same language. For example, the use of the sound sequence *mara* for denoting a tree in Kannada is not conditioned by the use of the sound sequence *giḍa* for denoting a plant (or by the use of any other sequence in that language), except that the two generally may not be identical in form. That is, a given sound–meaning relationship, occurring in a language, is basically independent of any other such relationship occurring in that same language.

Speakers of a language are not completely free, however, to use any sound or sound sequence to convey a given meaning. They have to follow a tradition in this respect, and in each language such traditions are handed down from one generation to the next. Thus, languages are able to maintain their individuality through time, and their speakers are able to understand each other even while using such arbitrary symbols. It is true that the speakers have a certain amount of freedom to rebel against the established traditions of their language. They can introduce new sound–meaning relationships in their language through lexical innovations (though these would be extremely limited in quantity). They can also borrow sound–meaning relationships from neighbouring languages and replace existing ones with such borrowings.

Such additions and replacements of sound–meaning relationships take place in all natural languages. As a result, the underlying tradition of sound–meaning relationships becomes more and more complex from a diachronic point of view. It is generally possible to divide the tradition of a language into a number of sub-traditions, each having its own line of development. For example, the study of sound–meaning relationships occurring in Kannada would reveal that they fall into several sub-traditions such as the Dravidian, Indo-Aryan (Sanskrit), Indo-European (English), Perso-Arabic, and so on. Among these, the Dravidian sub-tradition would be the most basic or inherited sub-tradition for this language, and the remaining ones would be its borrowed sub-traditions.

Diachronically, the inherited sub-tradition would appear as the core tradition around which more and more layers of sub-traditions have been added through borrowings and innovations. This core tradition would also be getting reduced continuously. The distinction between the inherited and non-inherited sub-traditions of sound–meaning relationship, however, cannot be taken as absolute as far as the diachronic study of a language is concerned. This is because there is no period in which such additions or replacements of relationships were completely absent. In fact, such processes of additions and replacements can theoretically be traced back to the time when double articulation itself was being formulated as the basic structure of sound–meaning relationship. That is, they can be traced back to the very beginning of language.

Hence the diachronic study of a language has to make use of the distinction between inherited and non-inherited sub-traditions of sound–meaning relationship only in relation to the point of time from which the line of development of a given set of languages is to be worked out. In the case of Dravidian languages, for example, one can separate borrowings and other innovative additions that were made in their respective traditions only *after* they had separated from a common point, namely Proto-Dravidian. Any borrowings or innovations of sound–meaning relationships that might have taken place *prior* to their separation from this common Proto-Dravidian stage cannot be considered as forming distinct non-inherited sub-traditions, but only as part of the inherited sub-tradition.

Such a procedure is fruitful in diachronic linguistics because the distinction between inherited and non-inherited traditions of sound–meaning relationships is relevant only for the diachronic study of a given language. It is irrelevant as far as its functioning as a code of communication is concerned, except in certain special cases where the addition of a sub-tradition has taken place rather recently. It is also mostly irrelevant for the occurrence of sound changes or other types of language changes. For these latter purposes, both inherited and non-inherited traditions behave as a unified single tradition.

For example, the Tappu dialect of Koraga (a Dravidian language) has undergone a change of initial *p* to *h*. This change has not taken place in the Onti dialect of Koraga. In Tappu, the change has affected not only the words that have been inherited by it, but also words that it has apparently borrowed from Tulu (see 6 a, b). On the other hand, Tulu has not changed its initial *p* to *h*.

(6a) *Change of initial p to h occurring in inherited words*:

| *Gloss* | *Onti* | *Tappu* |
|---|---|---|
| catch | *puḍḍu* | *huḍɨ* |
| outside | *pedmayi* | *hidmayi* |
| shake | *pandɨ* | *handɨ* |
| bag, basket | *piṭare* | *hiḍke* |
| behind | *peravu* | *heravu* |

(6b) *Change of initial p to h occurring in borrowed words*:

| *Gloss* | *Tulu* | *Tappu* |
|---|---|---|
| festival | *parba* | *harba* |
| cow | *petta* | *hetta* |
| name | *pudarɨ* | *hudarɨ* |
| field rat | *perguḍɛ* | *herguḍɛ* |
| praise | *pugarɨ* | *hugarɨ* |
| eleven | *pattonji* | *hattonji* |

When we apply comparative method to words drawn from a given set of languages, we generally restrict ourselves to the inherited set of lexical items, because these represent, very clearly, the various sound changes that have affected the languages as they developed from the proto-language. Lexical items belonging to non-inherited sub-traditions are to be separated from this inherited sub-tradition for this purpose. The term "cognate" is used for referring to these inherited words that are shared by two or more daughter languages.

### 4.2.1 PHONETIC DISTINCTIONS AND SETS OF OPPOSITIONS

Basic to this relationship between sounds and meanings is the distinction between the sounds themselves. Each language has its own limited set of phonetic distinctions which it uses either singly or in various combinations in order to differentiate between sequences of sounds.

These sequences of sounds, in their turn, are used by the language for conveying different meanings. For example, Hindi uses the *p/b* distinction singly to differentiate between pairs of meaningful sequences such as the following:

| (7a) | *Hindi* | *Gloss* | *Hindi* | *Gloss* |
|---|---|---|---|---|
| | *pi:r* | 'old' | *bi:r* | 'brave' |
| | *pa:lak* | 'spinach' | *ba:lak* | 'boy' |
| | *pal* | 'moment' | *bal* | 'force' |
| | *panjar* | 'skeleton' | *banjar* | 'barren' |
| | *pacna:* | 'be digested' | *bacna:* | 'be saved' |

Hindi also uses the *p/b* distinction in combination with other phonetic distinctions such as *t/d*, *n/t* and *ṛ/ḍh* in pairs of words such as the following respectively:

| (7b) | *Hindi* | *Gloss* | *Hindi* | *Gloss* |
|---|---|---|---|---|
| | *pota:* | 'grandson' | *boda:* | 'timid' |
| | *patni:* | 'wife' | *batti:* | 'wick' |
| | *paṛna:* | 'fall' | *baṛhna:* | 'grow' |

We may quantify this type of differentiation, occurring between meaningful sequences of sounds, through the use of the term "opposition" as follows: When two items (sequences of sounds) are differentiated from one another by a single phonetic distinction, as for example in the pair of words *pi:r* 'old' vs. *bi:r* 'brave', we may consider them as containing a single opposition. On the other hand, when two items are differentiated from one another jointly by two different phonetic distinctions, as in the case of words *paṛna:* 'fall' vs. *baṛhna:* 'grow' (or by the same distinction occurring twice as in *la:l* 'red' vs. *pa:p* 'sin'), we may consider them as containing two oppositions, and so on.

We may also list all the oppositions that a particular phonetic distinction represents in a given language and consider them together as forming a "set of oppositions". For example, the *p/b* distinction is used in Hindi to represent a set of oppositions which includes those found in pairs of words like *pi:r* : *bi:r* given above, and also those found in many others. Thus a set of oppositions can be defined as one that is represented by a single phonetic distinction in a given language.

The use of the term "recurring correspondences" roughly corresponds to the above definition of a "set of oppositions", but the term "correspondence" is also used to refer to phonetic distinctions. Hence its use in the present context will not help us in our effort to differentiate between sets of oppositions on the one hand and phonetic distinctions that represent them on the other. The use of the term "contrast" or "set of contrasts" would also lead to similar difficulties.

### 4.2.2 NATURE OF PHONETIC DISTINCTIONS

Our discussion has so far taken phonetic distinctions to be segmental. This, however, need not necessarily be the case. They can as well be described in terms of distinctive features, or the traditional phonemes. Depending upon the basic unit of phonetic distinctions that we choose, the size of the set of oppositions that they are to represent would vary. The choice does not appear to have any other relevance to our study of the reconstruction of sound changes. However, care must be taken to see that descriptions are based throughout on one single interpretation of the term "phonetic distinction".

There are two interesting points that deserve our attention in this context. First, the distinctive feature analysis *selects* the set of features that are relevant in a language, and discards those that are predictable and therefore irrelevant. For the study of sound change, however, both predictable as well as non-predictable features are relevant. This is because the loss of a non-predictable feature can turn a predictable feature into a non-predictable one. In Old Kannada, for example, nasalization of vowels occurring before a word-final nasal was apparently a predictable feature, but in some of its modern dialects, the loss of the word-final nasal has turned it into a non-predictable feature. The following pairs of Havyaka words exemplify this change:

| (8) | *Gloss* | *Old Kannada* | *Havyaka* |
|---|---|---|---|
| | he came | *bandan* | *bandã* |
| | she came | *bandaḷ* | *banda* |
| | he | *avan* | *avã* |
| | she | *avaḷ* | *ava* |
| | he won't go | *po:gan* | *ho:gã* |
| | she won't go | *po:gaḷ* | *ho:ga* |

It is possible, perhaps, to argue, in view of this relevance of even predictable or irrelevant features for the study of sound change, that the predictable and non-predictable features together function as a single phonetic distinction, representing a single set of oppositions in a given language. That is, in the above case, the contrast in Old Kannada was not merely between word-final *n* and *ḷ*, but rather between (a) *n* along with the nasalization that occurs on the preceding vowel on the one hand, and (b) *ḷ* on the other. This would account for the fact that the loss of one of them (*n* in the above case) does not affect the set of oppositions as such. The set continues to be represented by the remaining feature (namely the nasalized vowel in the above case).

The second point that needs to be noted here is that the traditional phonemic analysis *identifies* phonemes by grouping together phones that are phonetically similar and are in complementary distribution (i.e. allophones). The studies of sound changes have so far failed to show the relevance of such groupings for an understanding of their history. For example, a phonemic analysis would identify the voiceless stop *k* occurring before *i* as well as *u* (and also before other vowels and consonants) as constituting a single phoneme, namely *k*. However, in the case of Telugu, the former has changed into *c* whereas the latter (i.e. the one occurring before *u*) has remained unchanged as can be seen in the following Telugu realizations of proto-forms:

| (9) | *Gloss* | *Proto-form* | *Telugu* |
|---|---|---|---|
| | small | ***kiṟu*** | *ciṟu* |
| | parrot | ***kiḷi*** | *ciluka* |
| | be strewn | ***kintu*** | *cintu* |

| *Gloss* | *Proto-form* | *Telugu* |
|---|---|---|
| verdigris | **kilumu* | *cilumu* |
| heap | **kuppai* | *kuppa* |
| join | **ku:ṭu* | *ku:ḍu* |
| burn inside | **kumulu* | *kumulu* |
| leg | **ka:l* | *ka:lu* |

It may not be possible, on the other hand, to discard completely all the instances of identification as diachronically irrelevant. Sound changes do respect some instances of identification, as shown by the change of *k* to *c* in Telugu both before the vowel *i* as well as before the vowel *e*. Examples for this latter change (i.e. before *e*) are the following:

| *Gloss* | *Proto-form* | *Telugu* |
|---|---|---|
| scatter | **ketaṟ* | *cedaṟu* |
| ear | **kevi* | *cevi* |
| be spoiled | **keṭu* | *ceḍu* |

Notice, however, that the identification involved here is only of two different environments. It may or may not be a phonemically relevant identification. There is apparently a need to have a better understanding of the so-called "environment" of change that would lead to a more balanced postulation regarding the value of identification for the study of sound change. In the meantime, however, it is necessary to see that aspects of phonemic identification do not interfere with our understanding of the underlying processes of change, especially when traditional phonemes are used as units of phonetic distinctions.

### 4.2.3 REGULARITY AND IRREVERSIBILITY

Various diachronic studies of languages with known histories reveal that phonetic distinctions occurring in them did not undergo changes in a haphazard fashion. Though one finds much irregularity when related languages are compared, there are always underlying regularities of correspondence which come to the forefront when inherited items are separated from those that have been borrowed or individually altered. Such regularities of sound changes formed the main basis of the phenomenal success of comparative method in linguistics.

The reason for the existence of such regularities in the occurrence of sound changes can be seen in their incidence in language. As pointed out earlier (2.2), the occurrence of sound change, under normal circumstances, is restricted to the acquisitional age of a given generation of speakers. That is, the changes are caused by the fact that each new generation has to acquire its language by being exposed to the speech of its predecessors. It has to formulate the system of sounds purely on the basis of what or how the predecessors speak. Hence, each new generation is bound to develop differences in pronunciation, and these differences in effect form the sound changes that take place in the history of that language.

Thus, sound changes are changes that occur in the acquisition of the system of sounds as such, and not of individual words in which the sounds themselves occur. This accounts for the underlying regularity of those changes. Exceptions to this regularity are taken care of by the fact that grammar-oriented changes, borrowings and innovations taking place in the post-acquisitional period in a given generation would generally go against the results of such acquisitional changes.

The second important characteristic of sound changes, as mentioned earlier (see 2.3.2), is its irreversibility. That is, once a sound change has taken place in a language as a result of differences occurring between two generations in their acquisition of the system of sounds, no subsequent change (i.e. change occurring through acquisition in one of the following generations) can reverse it and bring back the earlier state of affairs.

The reason for this irreversibility of sound changes can be seen in the "scattering effect" that they have on groups of lexical items. A sound can bind together a number of lexical items that are otherwise unrelated. Consider the following two sets of Kannada words, of which the first one forms a group merely because all the words included in it begin with the sound *h*. They contrast minimally with the corresponding words occurring in the second set, which do not contain this initial *h* (see 10).

(10)

| Set I | | Set II | |
|---|---|---|---|
| *Kannada* | *Gloss* | *Kannada* | *Gloss* |
| *hakki* | 'bird' | *akki* | 'rice' |
| *huḷi* | 'sour' | *uḷi* | 'chisel' |
| *he:ḷu* | 'say' | *e:ḷu* | 'get up' |
| *hagga* | 'rope' | *agga* | 'cheap' |
| *hancu* | 'tile' | *ancu* | 'border' |
| *ha:ḍu* | 'sing' | *a:ḍu* | 'play' |
| *ha:ru* | 'fly' | *a:ru* | 'six' |
| *ha:lu* | 'milk' | *a:lu* | 'potato' |
| *ha:ḷu* | 'bad' | *a:ḷu* | 'person'. |

Notice that the lexical items of set I do not have any other similarity among them, either morphological or semantic, that can form the basis of such a grouping. The only common factor is the sharing of the initial sound *h*. If this initial *h* is deleted from all these words through a sound change, as has actually happened in the history of several Kannada dialects (as for example in the Okkaliga dialect of Mysore), all those lexical items would be "scattered" throughout the lexicon. Nothing would remain in them that could be used by the speakers of a following generation to bring them back into a single set at a later stage and differentiate them from the words of set II. This scattering effect of sound change on lexical items makes the change irreversible.

The basis of both these characteristics of sound change is evidently the double articulation that underlies the use of sounds in language. There is no direct relationship between sounds and meanings. As we have seen earlier (4.2), sounds are used to build forms and also to distinguish them from one another. These forms in turn are utilized for indicating different meanings. The indirect relationships so developed between sounds and meanings are arbitrary and tradition-bound. Speakers of a language have practically no choice in deciding as to what sounds or combinations of sounds they must utilize for indicating a given meaning. What little choice they may have in coining new forms to represent old or even newly discovered meanings has practically no effect on the system of sounds as such. This is because the system is vast and complex, and the number of forms traditionally available in a language–constructed from a comparatively small set of sounds–is very large.

Thus, the speakers of a language have to memorize its system of sounds and meanings. They do not generally make any conscious alterations in the sound–meaning relationships of their language because they have no motivation for doing so. Further, most of them are not even aware of these relationships, which, as we have seen above, are indirect. Any major changes that affect these relationships are due to differences in the acquisition of the sound system by successive generations of speakers.

The only exceptions to this are certain special cases of "heavy" borrowings (from neighbouring dialects or from earlier stages) which could bring back some of the lost sets of sound–meaning relationships into the language. If such borrowings are recent, they can easily be detected and separated from inherited items. On the other hand, if the borrowings were ancient, they would form part of the inherited sub-system itself, and would therefore fall outside the scope of the reconstruction procedure.

## 4.3 Procedures of reconstruction

As I have mentioned earlier (see 4.1.3), it would be easier to evaluate reconstructions if the exact procedures that are used to arrive at them, and the principles and hypotheses that have formed the basis of those procedures are specified. The two general terms that linguists use for referring to reconstruction procedures, namely comparative method and the method of internal reconstruction, actually consist of several such procedures each, which vary widely from one another in their reliability. This is mainly because the underlying hypotheses also vary widely in their validity. In the following sections some of these procedures and also the hypotheses on which they have been based are examined.

### 4.3.1 reconstructing a set of oppositions

One of the most important characteristics of sets of oppositions is that the speakers of a natural language cannot newly invent them. Further, if an existing set of oppositions is lost (due to the obliteration of a phonetic distinction that represented it earlier), it cannot be reintroduced into that language through sound changes that occur at a later stage (see 4.2.3). We can formulate a reconstruction procedure on the basis of this important characteristic of sets of oppositions. If the comparison of two languages indicates that one of them shows a set of oppositions that the other one does not, we can claim that the latter must have possessed it at an earlier stage, and must have lost it as a result of a sound change.

This reconstruction procedure forms part of the comparative method (see 4.1.1), but the latter makes use of several other procedures as well. Since we can be very sure about the validity of the hypothesis upon which this particular procedure has been based, we can consider it to be highly reliable. We can also consider it to be recovering "reality" as far as the sets of oppositions of the parent language are concerned. That is, the reconstruction that we can obtain through this procedure is not just a speculative assumption. The validity of the hypothesis upon which it is based has been repeatedly proved by several diachronic studies of languages belonging to different language families and spoken in different parts of the world.

It is necessary to mention one important point in this context. Notice that the above procedure is incapable of recovering the actual phonetic distinction that represented the reconstructed set of oppositions in the parent language. This is because the hypothesis that underlies this procedure does not say anything about changes that affect phonetic distinctions as such. A given phonetic distinction may get partially obliterated, leaving the set of oppositions represented by it intact, and in such instances, the procedure cannot be used for recovering an earlier stage.

For example, the loss of word-final *n* in Havyaka (see 8 of 4.2.2) was a partial obliteration of a phonetic distinction. While the nasal/non-nasal distinction was obliterated in the word-final position, the accompanying nasalized/oral distinction, occurring in the preceding vowel, was retained intact. As a result, the set of oppositions that the former distinction represented in the earlier stage was merely shifted to this latter distinction. Since there had been no loss of the concerned set of oppositions, the above-mentioned reconstruction procedure would not be applicable in the case of such changes. That is, even though Havyaka differs from Standard Kannada in having a phonetic distinction between oral and nasalized vowels that is absent in Standard Kannada, we cannot make use of the above-mentioned procedure and claim that the earlier stage did possess such a distinction.

The point to be noted here is that there is an important distinction between a set of oppositions on the one hand, and the phonetic or phonemic distinction—the so-called "contrast"—which represents it on the other. It is only the former that gets reconstructed when we apply the procedure mentioned above. Its underlying hypothesis is only about sets of oppositions and not about phonetic distinctions or contrasts.

Supposing we compare two different languages, and find that a contrast (or phonetic distinction) of one language corresponds to the absence of any contrast in another language. We cannot categorically claim that the parent language was like the former language in manifesting the contrast and that the latter language had lost that contrast. There can actually be two different types of situations in which such a correspondence would become available, and only one of them may involve the loss of a set of oppositions.

(a) Merger of two different sounds

The first possibility is that the situation might have resulted from the merger of two different sounds. For example, the retroflex and alveolar nasals (**n* and **ṇ*) of the parent language have merged into *n* in Telugu, but not in Kannada. As a result, the *ṇ~n* phonetic distinction (or contrast) that occurs in Kannada is absent in Telugu. There is also a corresponding loss of a set of oppositions (namely the one represented by the distinction between the two merged sounds) in Telugu. In situations of this type, we can apply the above-mentioned procedure and recover the lost set of oppositions.

| (11) | *Gloss* | *Kannada* | *Telugu* |
|---|---|---|---|
| | earth | *maṇṇu* | *mannu* |
| | gold | *honnu* | *ponnu* |
| | eye | *kaṇṇu* | *kannu* |
| | eat | *tinnu* | *tinu* |
| | span | *ge:ṇu* | *ge:nu* |
| | louse | *he:nu* | *pe:nu* |

It may be convenient to represent this lost set of oppositions in our reconstruction of the parent language through a phonetic distinction that is identical with the one occurring in the language (such as Kannada) that has not undergone the merger. Notice, however, that this latter reconstruction (of the actual phonetic distinction of the parent language) does not result from the application of the reconstruction procedure mentioned above. One would have to postulate a different reconstruction procedure, based upon a different underlying hypothesis, for that purpose.

The following forms of Hindi and Punjabi provide another example for this loss of contrast through merger, leading to the loss of a set of oppositions. Sanskrit equivalents of these forms are also given below, which indicate the correctness of the suggested reconstruction.

| (12) | *Gloss* | *Hindi* | *Punjabi* | *Sanskrit* |
|---|---|---|---|---|
| (ia) | seven | *sa:t* | *satt* | *sapta* |
| (ib) | night | *ra:t* | *ra:t* | *ra:tri* |
| (iia) | fire | *a:g* | *agg* | *agni* |
| (iib) | manure | *kha:d* | *kha:d* | *kha:dya* |
| (iiia) | mother-in-law | *sa:s* | *sass* | *švašru:* |
| (iiib) | heap | *ra:s* | *ra:s* | *ra:ši* |
| (iva) | modesty | *la:j* | *lajj* | *lajja:* |
| (ivb) | seed | *bi:j* | *bi:j* | *bi:ja* |
| (va) | hand | *ha:th* | *hatth* | *hasta* |
| (vb) | wood | *ka:ṭh* | *ka:ṭh* | *ka:ṣṭha* |

Notice that in the case of both (a) and (b) forms, Hindi shows a long vowel in the first syllable, which is followed by a single consonant in both these cases. Punjabi, on the other hand, shows a short vowel in the case of (a) forms and a long vowel in the case of (b) forms. The former is followed by a long (or geminated) consonant whereas the latter is followed by a single consonant. That is, the distinction between long vowels and short vowels (or between geminated consonants and single consonants), occurring in Punjabi in this particular type of word structure, is missing in Hindi. The set of oppositions that is represented by this distinction in Punjabi is also missing in Hindi.

We may apply the procedure mentioned above in this case also and reconstruct the lost set of oppositions for the proto-language. The corresponding forms of Sanskrit given above indicate, however, that it would not be possible to reconstruct the actual phonetic detail that the parent language apparently possessed merely by comparing Hindi and Punjabi forms. There were consonant clusters after both short as well as long vowels in some of them, and in others there were single consonants. These distinctions have been lost in Punjabi as well.

(b) Split of a sound into two different sounds

The second possibility is that the above-mentioned type of correspondence (i.e. a situation in which a contrast that occurs in one language is missing in another language) can result from an entirely different type of sound change as well, namely the split of a sound into two different sounds. That is, the language that shows the contrast might have developed it later, by splitting what was earlier a single sound into two different sounds. Since changes of this type would not involve the loss of any sets of oppositions, they would not be amenable to the present reconstruction procedure. For example, Marathi has developed a contrast between *s* and *š* as result of a split, which is absent in Hindi.

The *s*~*š* contrast that occurred in Sanskrit had been lost in Prakrit, and hence it is unavailable both in Marathi as well as Hindi. However, a split has occurred in the history of Marathi as a result of which the sound *s* changed to *š* when it occurred before *i* or *y*, but remained as *s* in other contexts. (The change also occurred, though optionally, when the vowel *e* followed it.) The phonetic distinction that was introduced into the language through this split was apparently allophonic to start with, but as a result of borrowings it has become contrastive.

| (13a) | *Gloss* | *Marathi* | *Hindi* |
|---|---|---|---|
| | head | *šir* | *sir* |
| | horn | *šĩ:g* | *sĩ:g* |
| | sprinkle | *šĩcṇeĩ* | *sĩ:cna:* |
| | needle | *su:i* | *su:i:* |
| | sugar | *sa:kar* | *sakkar* |
| | gold | *sonẽ* | *sona:* |

Notice that the contrast that derives from a split is different from the one that derives from a merger. The former does not represent a set of oppositions by itself in cognate words. Languages do not split a sound paradigmatically, that is in the *same* environment. Split is basically a syntagmatic process. It affects sounds occurring in *different* environments, as is the case, for example, in the above-mentioned change. The sound *s* of the earlier stage has changed into *š* in one environment (before *i* or *y*) and has remained as *s* in other environments and thereby has given rise to a split. The following sets of words occurring in Marathi itself exemplify this situation:

| (13b) | *Marathi* | *Gloss* | *Marathi* | *Gloss* |
|---|---|---|---|---|
| | *divəs* | 'day' | *divš-i* | 'on the day' |
| | *ləs* | 'vaccine' | *ləš-i* | 'vaccines' |
| | *ghəsa* | 'throat' | *ghəš-yat* | 'in the throat' |

Since contrasts developing as a result of such splits do not involve the loss of any sets of oppositions, we cannot apply the present procedure of reconstruction to situations in which two languages differ from one another in showing a contrast that has developed from a split.

It may be noted here that contrasts may also be introduced into a language through borrowing. For example, the *s-š* contrast that had been lost earlier, was introduced into Hindi later on through borrowings from Sanskrit (see 6 of 2.4.1). However, since these borrowed items would be set aside before we apply our reconstruction procedures to languages, they need not be considered here.

### 4.3.2 PRINCIPLE OF PHONEMIC IDENTIFICATION

While reconstructing the proto-forms of Kannada, Tamil and Telugu through comparative method (see 4.1.1), it was suggested that the initial consonant of contrasts 1, 2, 3, 7 and 10 go back to **k*, whereas that of contrasts 12, 14 and 15 go back to **c*. This procedure allows us only to claim that the set of oppositions that the distinction represents in Kannada (but not in Tamil and Telugu) must have occurred in the proto-language. We need a different reconstruction procedure in order to *identify* one of the sounds involved with **k* (which occurs in cognates like 4, 5 and 6) and the other one with **c* (which occurs in cognates like 13). This point will become clear if we restrict ourselves only to the following sets of words of Kannada and Tamil and study the reconstruction of their initial consonant:

| (14) | *Gloss* | *Kannada* | *Tamil* |
|---|---|---|---|
| 2. | small | *kiṟu* | *ciṟu* |
| 9. | join | *ku:ḍu* | *ku:ṭu* |
| 12. | be entangled | *sikku* | *cikku* |
| 13. | wind | *suttu* | *cuṟṟu* |

These sets of words provide four different correspondences as shown below (and also a few others that are not relevant):

(i) *k* of Kannada corresponding to *c* of Tamil before front vowel.

(ii) *k* of Kannada corresponding to *k* of Tamil before back vowel.

(iii) *s* of Kannada corresponding to *c* of Tamil before front vowel.

(iv) *s* of Kannada corresponding to *c* of Tamil before back vowel.

It is true that the last two correspondences, (iii) and (iv), are generally viewed as representing a single proto-sound, but this assumption or reconstruction is based upon the principle of phonemic identification. As far as the reconstruction procedure given in 4.3.1 is concerned, we can only claim that the two pairs of correspondences, (i) -- (iii) and (ii) -- (iv) cannot be regarded as representing single proto-sounds. It provides no basis for the claim that (i) and (iv) cannot be grouped together, especially in view of the fact that Tamil has the same sound *c* in both of them.

The reconstruction procedure that is available in this latter case is the one based upon the principle of phonemic identification, involving notions like phonetic similarity and complementary distribution. In the present case, for example, it can be claimed, on the basis of that principle, that identifying (iii) with (iv) is preferable because none of the languages differentiate between the two. Hence we are left with the identification of (i) with (ii). However, the relevance of this principle of phonemic identification for the reconstruction of sound changes is yet to be established. As mentioned earlier (4.2.2), studies of sound changes have so far failed to bring out any facts that can support the claim that the principle is relevant for such a study.

### 4.3.3 NATURAL DIRECTION OF CHANGE

Another interesting procedure (or rather sets of procedures) that can form the basis of reconstruction concerns the notion of the "naturalness" of postulated sound changes. Studies of languages and dialects with recorded histories have shown that sound changes generally occur in fixed directions. It has been possible to establish some assumptions and hypotheses in this regard, as pointed out in the second chapter (see 2.6) and these can form the basis for a procedure to recover some of the phonological aspects of proto-forms.

For example, nasals are generally found to influence the neighbouring vowels and to change them into nasalized vowels. When a nasal is deleted, we therefore find the set of oppositions represented by the nasal/non-nasal consonant distinction being shifted to the neighbouring nasalized-oral vowel distinction. This generalization can form the basis of a reconstruction procedure, in that a correspondence between oral vowel + nasal and nasalized vowel can be assumed to develop from an earlier stage in which only the former (oral vowel + nasal) occurred and not the other way round. We can apply this procedure of reconstruction to Havyaka words that have nasalized vowels (see 8 of 4.2.2) and claim that the earlier stage had an oral vowel + nasal sequence in those words.

Another example for this reconstruction procedure is the *k/c* correspondence occurring between Kannada and Tamil (and also Telugu) described earlier. We assumed that this correspondence results from the change of **k* to *c* before front vowels in Tamil and Telugu, rather than from the change of **c* to *k* in Kannada in the same environment. This reconstruction is based upon the hypothesis that it is more natural for *k* to get palatalized rather than for *c* to get depalatalized when followed by front vowels. Palatalization is one of the frequently occurring changes that allow reconstruction on the basis of this naturalness assumption.

Notice, however, that generalizations that this reconstruction procedure can make use of are all based upon *tendencies* of change. Hence reconstructions established on the basis of this procedure are not as valid as the ones obtained through the use of the first procedure mentioned above, namely the recovery of a lost set of oppositions. Further, different hypotheses that form the bases of this procedure would have different degrees of validity. For example, the validity of the hypothesis concerning nasalized vowels may not be the same as the one concerning the palatalization of velar consonants. The evaluation of a particular reconstruction based upon this procedure of natural direction of sound change would therefore depend upon the validity of the particular hypothesis used.

### 4.3.4 MAJORITY RULE

The exact phonetic value of a reconstructed sound is generally unavailable. For example, if *c* of one language corresponds to *s* of another language in all environments, it would be difficult to determine the phonetic value of the corresponding sound in the proto-language. However, linguists do make use of certain reconstruction procedures in such contexts. One of them is based upon what is called "the majority rule".

According to this procedure, if one language diverges from several others in correspondence, the proto-form is considered to have been more like what the majority of the surviving languages show. It would be interesting to see whether this assumption is universally valid. One might examine it from the point of view of language families with known histories, and see whether a majority of daughter languages or dialects in each such history do join together in retaining the phonetic value of the sounds of the earlier language. Even if proved correct (which appears very unlikely), the validity of this purely statistical procedure differs vastly from that of the first procedure mentioned in (4.3.1).

### 4.3.5 PRINCIPLE OF ECONOMY

The application of some of the procedures described above, such as that of phonemic identification, may sometimes give rise to several competing solutions. When faced with such multiplicity of solutions, linguists make use of a procedure based upon the principle of economy for selecting one out of those competing solutions. They choose the solution that reconstructs the least number of phonemes for the proto-language, or the one that sets up the smallest number of steps for deriving the daughter languages from the reconstructed proto-language.

The point to be noted here is that any doubt regarding the validity of these principles or hypotheses affects only the reconstructions that have been obtained through procedures that are directly based upon them, and not the reconstructions that have been obtained through other procedures.

### 4.3.6 ADDITIONAL PROCEDURES

One can think of several other procedures of this nature for reconstructing earlier stages of a given set of genetically related languages. For example, Hoenigswald (1960: 99) suggests that an observation regarding the relative frequency of the occurrence of sounds can be used for this purpose. It has been observed that in a universe of ten thousand sounds of continuous text in ten different Sanskrit passages of one thousand words each, *a* occurs with a frequency of 19.78 per cent, while the next ranking segmental phoneme occurs less than half as frequently as that. This disparity in the relative frequency of the sounds of Sanskrit can be utilized for assuming that the vowel *a* of Sanskrit has resulted from the merger of two or more vowels of the proto-language.

We can regard this statistical procedure of reconstruction as forming part of the method of internal reconstruction because it makes use of data from a single language. Comparison of Sanskrit with other Indo-European languages such as Latin and Greek (i.e. the application of comparative method) provides support for this statistical procedure of reconstruction, as can be seen from the following examples:

| (15) | *Gloss* | *Sanskrit* | *Latin* |
|---|---|---|---|
| Set I: | | | |
| 1. | metal | *ayas* | *aes* |
| 2. | away | *apa* | *ab* |
| 3. | goose | *hamsa* | *anser* |
| 4. | fall | *šad-* | *cadit* |
| Set II: | | | |
| 5. | is | *asti* | *es* |
| 6. | horse | *ašva* | *eques* |
| 7. | old | *sana* | *senex* |
| 8. | middle | *madhya* | *medius* |
| Set III: | | | |
| 9. | sheep | *avi* | *ovis* |
| 10. | work | *apas* | *opus* |
| 11. | bone | *asthi* | *os* |
| 12. | husband | *pati* | *potis* 'able' |

Notice that the vowel *a* of Sanskrit corresponds to Latin *a* in the first set of cognates (1–4), whereas in the second (5–8) and third (9–12) sets of cognates it corresponds to Latin *e* and *o*, respectively. By applying the first procedure mentioned above (recovering the lost set of oppositions), we can claim that the parent language was like Latin rather than like Sanskrit as far as the vowel *a* of Sanskrit is concerned.

It is thus evident that the number of distinct procedures that are available for reconstructing sound changes would depend upon the number of generalizations and hypotheses that we can establish regarding the effects of sound change on language. The validity of individual aspects of reconstruction that we obtain through these procedures would also depend directly upon the validity of the generalizations and hypotheses upon which those procedures have been based.

## 4.4 Summary

The two prominent methods of reconstruction, called internal and comparative, actually involve several different procedures of reconstruction, each based upon a different hypothesis regarding the effect of sound change on language. In order to satisfactorily evaluate the results of our reconstructions, we need to examine them from the point of view of individual procedures used, and also from that of the hypotheses upon which they have been established. We have examined the reliability of some of the procedures of this nature on the basis of the reliability of the hypotheses that underlie them.

### Further readings

1. Regarding comparative method, see
   Hoenigswald 1960. *Language change and linguistic reconstruction.*
   Lehmann 1963. *Historical linguistics* ch. 5.
   Bloomfield 1933. *Language* ch. 18.
   Bhat 1975a. *The basis of comparative method.*
   Anderson 1973. *Structural aspects of language change,* ch. 3.
   Anttila 1972. *An introduction to historical and comparative method* ch. 10, 11.
2. Regarding internal reconstruction, see
   Hoenigswald 1960. *Language change and linguistic reconstruction.*
   Lehman 1963. *Historical linguistics* ch. 5.
   Miranda 1975. *Internal reconstruction: scope and limits.*
   Kuryłowicz 1964. *On the methods of internal reconstruction.*
   Marchand 1956. *Internal reconstruction of phonemic split.*
   Chafe 1959. *Internal reconstruction in Seneca.*
3. Regarding other procedures of reconstruction, see
   Bonfante 1945. *On reconstruction and linguistic method.*
4. Regarding the evaluation of reconstructions, see
   Pulgram 1959. *Proto-Indo-European reality and reconstruction.*
   Pulgram 1961. *The nature and use of proto-language.*
   Hoenigswald 1960. *Language change and linguistic reconstruction.*

# EXERCISES

## CHAPTER 1. Evidence for sound change

1. A comparison of two modern dialects of Tulu indicates that several words of the basic vocabulary show a contrast between *l* and *ḷ* in one dialect but not in the other dialect. Suppose that an excavation unearthed certain Tulu inscriptions belonging to the twelfth century AD and in those inscriptions the language used is similar to the second dialect in *not* showing the *l-ḷ* contrast in the words mentioned above. What would be your conclusion regarding the history of the two modern dialects? Would you derive both of them from the recorded form of the twelfth century? If so, how will you obtain the *l-ḷ* contrast of the first dialect?
2. Several claims have been made regarding the relationship between Dravidian languages and languages spoken outside India such as the Finno-Ugric and certain African languages. Similarities in the lexicon and grammar have been given in support of these claims. What type of additional proof is necessary in order to make these claims acceptable?
3. If a sound change has removed a distinction between two sounds, as has happened in the case of the distinction between *s* and *š* in Hindi, would it be possible for the speakers of that language to bring back that distinction as it existed earlier? Hindi does make a distinction between *s* and *š*. Would you say that it has *reversed* the earlier sound change?
4. What are the main differences between descriptive and comparative evidence? How do you reduce external evidence into comparative? Explain.

## CHAPTER 2. Characteristics of sound change

1. Sanskrit had undergone a sound change by which aspirated stops became de-aspirated when followed by another aspirated sound (see 2 of 3.3.2 for details). Later on Pali underwent other sound changes by which initial stop + sibilant and sibilant + stop clusters became aspirated stops. As a result of these latter changes, Pali came to have aspirated stops occurring before other aspirated stops as can be seen in the following examples:

| *Gloss* | *Sanskrit* | *Pali* |
|---|---|---|
| shoulder | *skandha* | *khandha* |
| prop | *skambha* | *khambha* |
| fixed firmly | *stabdha* | *thaddha* |
| pillar | *stambha* | *thambha* |
| agitation | *kṣobha* | *khobha* |

Would you say that the effect of the previous sound change has been "reversed" by the following sound changes in the history of Pali? Explain.

2. Here are a few sets of words belonging to Tamil and English (Southworth 1982). The words show some similarities and also some differences. Can you claim that the two languages are genetically related on the basis of these similarities? If not, can you give any specific reason why the two cannot be regarded as related?

| *Tamil* | | *English* |
|---|---|---|
| *oṉṟu* | 'one' | *one* |
| *eṭṭu* | 'eight' | *eight* |
| *aruvi* | 'brook' | *river* |
| *ellam* | 'all' | *all* |
| *ku:ṭu* | 'possible' | *could* |
| *paiyaṉ* | 'boy' | *boy* |

| *Tamil* | | *English* |
|---|---|---|
| *kol* | 'kill' | *kill* |
| *maṇi* | 'bead' | *money* |
| *katti* | 'knife' | *cutter* |
| *maṉai* | 'house' | *manor* |
| *kiṭai* | 'obtain' | *get* |
| *ve:ṇṭu* | 'want' | *want* |

3. Examine the following word forms of Boro and establish morphophonemic alternations for the stems and affixes in order to account for the variations in their forms. Describe the nature of the alternations that you have established.

| | | | |
|---|---|---|---|
| *zá* | 'to eat' | *zadéŋ* | 'he eats' |
| *ku* | 'to hit' | *kudeŋ* | 'he hits' |
| *zó* | 'to sit' | *pozó* | 'to seat' |
| *zo* | 'to tear' | *gozo* | 'torn' |
| *ná* | 'fish' | | |
| *kú* | 'thorn' | *nakú* | 'fish bone' |
| *hóm* | 'to catch hold of' | | |
| *tá* | 'to stop' | *homtá* | 'to put in custody' |
| *kú* | 'to prick' | | |
| *táb* | 'to paste' | *kutáb* | 'to sew together' |
| *buŋ* | 'to say' | | |
| *káŋ* | 'to bring up' | *buŋ káŋ* | 'to announce' |

## CHAPTER 3. Effects of sound change

1. You may try to gather examples for the various types of effects described in this chapter from your own language, or from a language that is known to you. This will give you a better understanding of the nature of these effects and the way in which they differ from one another.
2. There are several additional examples in the book itself for most of the changes that are described in this chapter. For example, No. (42) of this chapter, which describes the change of Havyaka *s* to *š* in Havyaka after front vowels can be an example for progressive (preservative) assimilation. No. (13) of Chapter 4, which describes the change of Marathi *s* to *š* that occurred before *i* and *y*, is an example for regressive (anticipatory) assimilation. Both are examples for partial assimilations. You may try to find additional examples for other types of changes as well. I have given an index of changes that are described in the book at various places in order to help you in doing this exercise (see appendix).
3. Examine the following two sets of verbal forms taken from Kudux:

| | | | |
|---|---|---|---|
| *erc* | 'to search' | *irchkan* | 'I searched' |
| *lebd* | 'to throw' | *libdkan* | 'I threw' |
| *alx* | 'to laugh' | *əlxkan* | 'I laughed' |
| *e:r* | 'to see' | *i:rkan* | 'I saw' |
| *o:g* | 'to swim' | *u:gkan* | 'I swam' |
| *olx* | 'to write' | *ulxkan* | 'I wrote' |
| *a:n* | 'to ask' | *ə:nkan* | 'I washed' |
| *paḍg* | 'to scold' | *pəḍgkan* | 'I scolded' |
| *mõ:ḍ* | 'to wash' | *muũ:ḍkan* | 'I washed' |
| *oŋkh* | 'to cough' | *uŋkhkan* | 'I coughed' |
| *me:x* | 'to call' | *mi:xkan* | 'I called' |
| *ṭa:ṭ* | 'to lick' | *ṭə:ṭkan* | 'I licked' |

Establish morphophonemic alternations that would be needed

to account for these sets of forms. What types of alternations have you established? Given that the following sets of verbal forms also occur in Kudux, what modifications do you wish to make in the classifications of those alternations?

| | | | |
|---|---|---|---|
| *nulx* | 'to swallow' | *nulxkan* | 'I swallowed' |
| *dobḍ* | 'to fold' | *dobḍkan* | 'I folded' |

4. Compare the Sanskrit and Sinhalese words given below. Postulate sound changes in order to account for the differences that occur between these two languages and classify the effects of those sound changes. You may neglect the final vowel of Sinhalese words.

| *Gloss* | *Sanskrit* | *Sinhalese* | |
|---|---|---|---|
| cock | *kukkuṭa* | *kukuḷa* | |
| leper | *kuṣṭin* | *kiḷi* | |
| hut | *kuṭi:ra* | *kiḷiya* | |
| misery | *duḥka* | *duka* | |
| ill-behaved | *duḥši:la* | *disil* | 'impious' |
| distant | *du:ra* | *dura* | |
| virtue | *puṇya* | *pina* | |
| town | *pura* | *pura* | |
| purity | *šuddhi* | *sidu* | |
| earth | *bhu:mi* | *bima* | |
| shaven | *muṇḍa* | *muḍa* | |
| foolish | *mu:ḍha* | *muḷu* | |
| price | *mu:lya* | *mila* | |
| blood | *rudhira* | *rihiri* | |
| dropped | *galita* | *gili* | |
| angry | *kupyati* | *kipi* | |
| cotton | *tu:li* | *tili* | 'mattress' |
| worship | *pu:ja:* | *puda* | |
| honored | *pu:jita* | *pidu* | |
| root | *mu:la* | *mula* | |

## CHAPTER 4. Reconstruction of sound change

1. In Old Tamil, disyllabic verbs ending in *l* can have their transitive/causative forms derived by adding the suffix *r̲u*. The verbs have a different stem form, namely one ending in the consonant *r̲*, when followed by this suffix.

| | | | |
|---|---|---|---|
| *akal* | 'to spread' | *akar̲r̲u* | 'to widen' |
| *aṛal* | 'to burn (intr.)' | *aṛar̲r̲u* | 'to burn (tr.)' |
| *iyal* | 'to be possible' | *iyar̲r̲u* | 'to effect' |
| *uṛal* | 'to oscillate' | *uṛar̲r̲u* | 'to drive to and fro' |
| *kaṛal* | 'to become loose' | *kaṛar̲r̲u* | 'to loosen' |
| *cuṛal* | 'to spin (intr.)' | *cuṛar̲r̲u* | 'to spin (tr.)' |
| *tuval* | 'to drip' | *tuvar̲r̲u* | 'to sprinkle' |
| *payil* | 'to get trained' | *payir̲r̲u* | 'to train' |
| *mural* | 'to cry' | *murar̲r̲u* | 'to make cry' |

Can you reconstruct the sound change that is responsible for this stem alternation? What procedure(s) of reconstruction do you use for this purpose? What are your reconstructed forms for the proto-stage?

2. Examine the Kudux verbal forms given below and establish morphophonemic alternations that occur in them. Reconstruct the earlier stage using the method of internal reconstruction.

| | | | |
|---|---|---|---|
| *e:dʔ* | 'to show' | *e:dkan* | 'I showed' |
| | | *e:dʔas* | 'He showed' |
| *pe:sʔ* | 'to order' | *pe:skan* | 'I ordered' |
| | | *pe:sʔan* | 'He ordered' |
| *pu:xʔ* | 'to boil' | *pu:xkan* | 'I boiled' |
| | | *pu:xʔan* | 'He boiled' |
| *tindʔ* | 'to eat' | *tindkan* | 'I ate' |
| | | *tindan* | 'He ate' |
| *mundʔ* | 'to close' | *mundkan* | 'I closed' |
| | | *mundʔan* | 'He closed' |
| *xoxʔ* | 'to wait' | *xoxkan* | 'I waited' |
| | | *xoxʔan* | 'He waited' |

3. Compare the following words of Hindi and Marathi and reconstruct proto-forms for each of them. What are the sound changes that you need to postulate in order to derive words of these two languages from the proto-forms?

| *Gloss* | *Hindi* | *Marathi* |
|---|---|---|
| barren | *bã:jh* | *vã:jh* |
| grow | *ba:ṛh* | *va:ṛh* |
| ledger | *bahi:* | *vahi:* |
| deaf | *bahira:* | *bahira:* |
| dam | *bã:dh* | *bã:dh* |
| fence | *ba:ṛ* | *va:ṛ* |
| dwelling | *ba:s* | *va:s* |
| much | *bahut* | *bahut* |
| scarse | *biral* | *viral* |
| marriage | *biva:h* | *viva:h* |
| hunger | *bhu:kh* | *bhu:kh* |
| warrior | *bi:r* | *vi:r* |

4. Examine the alternations shown by the verbal bases of Malto in the verbal forms given below. State the alternations involved and establish sound changes that might have caused these alternations.

| | | | |
|---|---|---|---|
| *piṭ* | 'to kill' | *piṭyah* | 'he killed' |
| *o:g* | 'to swim' | *ogyah* | 'he swam' |
| *ṭa:ṭ* | 'to lick' | *ṭaṭyah* | 'he licked' |
| *ca:d* | 'to select' | *cadyah* | 'he selected' |
| *e:k* | 'to go' | *ekyah* | 'he went' |
| *amb* | 'to leave' | *ambyah* | 'he left' |

5. Compare the following words of Kudux and Malto, reconstruct proto-forms and state the sound changes that are responsible for the differences that occur between the two languages in these words. The symbols *q* and *g* of Malto represent uvular voiceless stop and uvular voiced fricative, respectively.

| *Gloss* | *Kudux* | *Malto* |
|---|---|---|
| walk | *e:k* | *e:ke* |
| gather | *ba:k* | *ba:ke* |
| deer | *ma:k* | *ma:ku* |
| salt | *be:k* | *be:ku* |
| ant | *po:k* | *po:ku* |
| dig | *arx* | *arg̣e* |
| go to stool | *erx* | *erg̣e* |
| open | *calx* | *calg̣e* |
| trample | *tirx* | *tirg̣e* |
| sky | *merxa* | *merg̣u* |
| buffalo | *manxa* | *mang̣u* |
| head | *kukk* | *kuku* |
| sit | *okk* | *oke* |
| punch | *tukk* | *tuke* |
| prick | *cakh* | *caqe* |
| get | *xakh* | *qaqe* |
| come out | *urkh* | *urqe* |
| laugh | *alkh* | *alqe* |

# APPENDIX: LIST OF SOUND CHANGES

The following is a list of sound changes that have been given as examples in the book in different chapters. The first number indicates the chapter in which they occur and the second one, within brackets, denotes the number of the example.

1. Loss of contrast between short and long vowels in Hindi ch 1 (10), ch 4 (12).
2. Development of nasalized vowels from vowel + nasal sequences through loss of the nasal in Hindi ch 1 (12) and Havyaka ch 4 (8).
3. Development of tonal distinction in Punjabi as a result of the merger of aspirates with voiceless unaspirates ch 2 (2), ch 3 (52).
4. Loss of word-final vowels in Hindi ch 3 (50).
5. Loss of initial short vowels (i) when they are followed by a consonant which is short and is other than velar or labial, (ii) when the following vowel is short, and (iii) when a cluster follows that vowel, in Sapaliga Tulu ch 3 (2).
6. Loss of the second vowel of trisyllabic words of (c)vcvcv pattern in Mysore Kannada ch 3 (3).
7. Insertion of *i* between the two consonants of initial *sn* cluster in Pali ch 3 (8).
8. Addition of final *u* to words ending in a consonant in Kannada ch 3 (10).
9. Change of *ai* to *e* and *au* to *o* in Pali ch 3 (11).
10. Addition of a *w*-glide to words with an initial *o* or *o:* in Kannada ch 3 (7).
11. Change of *wo* to *wa* and *wo:* to *wa:* in Mysore Kannada ch 3 (7), ch 3 (12).
12. Change of *i* to *u* after bilabial sounds in Tulu ch 3 (16) and after

*p* in Sanketi Tamil ch 3 (23).

13. Change of *i* to *e* before the vowel *a* in Telugu ch 3 (22).
14. Change of *ɔ* to *o* before high vowels in Bengali ch 3 (25).
15. Change of *a* to *ə* before high vowels in Gulbarga Kannada ch 3 (26), ch 3 (53).
16. Change of *e* to *i* and *o* to *u* before high vowels in Kannada ch 1 (3), ch 3 (24).
17. Change of *e* to *i* before the vowel *a* in Tamil ch 3 (31).
18. Merger of the vowels *e*, *o* and *a* to *a* in Sanskrit ch 3 (38), ch 4 (15).
19. Change of the vowels *o* and *o:* to *a* and *a:* respectively, after the bilabial *m* in Bellari Kannada ch 3 (30).
20. Assimilation of vowels in certain prefixes to vowels of the following roots in Boro ch 3 (27).
21. Change of *k* to *c* before front vowels in Tamil and Telugu ch 3 (49), ch 4 (2), ch 4 (9) and ch 4 (14).
22. Change of *k* to *c* and *g* to *j* before front vowels in Hosur Kannada ch 1 (1).
23. Change of *s* to *c* in Kannada ch 4 (14).
24. Word-final *k* and *ṭ* to *j* in Sanskrit ch 3 (43).
25. Split of Indo-European $k^w$ to *k* and *c* in Sanskrit ch 3 (38).
26. Change of the consonant *d* to *j* before front vowels in Tulu ch 3 (18).
27. Change of the clusters *ty* to *cc* and *dy* to *jj* in Prakrit ch 3 (20).
28. Change of *f* to *v* medially in English ch 3 (41).
29. Change of *p* to *f* except after an initial *s* and of *b* to *p* in English ch 3 (37).
30. Change of *t* and *c* to *t*, *c*, *s*, *h* and *zero* in Tulu dialects ch 2 (10).
31. Change of *pt* to *tt* in Pali ch 3 (21).
32. Assimilation of *r* to the following stop in Kannada ch 3 (17).
33. Assimilation of *y* to the preceding consonant in Pali ch 3 (15).
34. Change of sibilants to *h* before nasals and change of place (metathesis) of the two in Prakrit ch 3 (34).
35. Change of *kh* to *h* medially in Prakrit ch 3 (36) and also of other aspirates like *th*, *dh* and *gh* ch 3 (19).
36. Devoicing of word-final *d* in Sanskrit ch 2 (4), ch 3 (40), ch 4 (4).
37. Devoicing of *b*, *d* and *g* before *p*, *t* and *k* in Boro ch 4 (3).

38. Devoicing of *g* in the word-final position in Kudali Marathi ch 3 (45).
39. Voicing of *c*, *k* and *t* when immediately preceded by a voiced sound and non-immediately by an aspirate in Manipuri ch 3 (32), ch 4 (5).
40. Loss of a consonant from clusters and compensatory lengthening of preceding vowel in Hindi ch 3 (6).
41. Loss of initial *k* occurring before nasals in English ch 3 (50).
42. Loss of word-final *t* in Pali ch 3 (5).
43. Loss of word-final consonants in Havyaka Kannada ch 3 (46).
44. Cluster reduction in Prakrit and Hindi ch 1 (7).
45. Loss of intervocalic stops in Prakrit ch 3 (4).
46. Gemination of stops in the third syllable of words of (c)vcvcv pattern in Havyaka Kannada ch 3 (9).
47. Change of *c* to *č* and *s* to *š* when followed by *i* and *y* in Marathi ch 1 (11), ch 4 (13).
48. Change of *s* to *š* when preceded by front vowels in Havyaka Kannada ch 3 (42).
49. Merger of *š* with *s* in Hindi ch 1 (5), ch 2 (6), ch 3 (47) and in Prakrit ch 2 (3).
50. Aspirated stops getting de-aspirated and *s* changed to *c* when preceded by an aspirated sound (including *s* and *h*) in Manipuri ch 3 (28), ch 3 (32), ch 4 (5).
51. Aspirated stops getting de-aspirated when followed by an aspirated sound in Sanskrit ch 3 (29).
52. Change of initial *p* to *h* in Tappu Koraga ch 4 (6).
53. Change of *p* to *h* in Kannada and loss of *h* in the Mysore dialect ch 1 (6), ch 3 (1), ch 3 (48), ch 4 (10).
54. Change of *ṇ* to *n* in Sapaliga Tulu ch 1 (2), ch 1 (9), in Telugu ch 4 (11) and in Hindi ch 3 (44).
55. Change of *n* to *ṇ* in Prakrit ch 3 (14).
56. Change of *ḷ* to *l* in Sapaliga Tulu ch 3 (35), ch 4 (1).
57. Change of *r̤* to *ḷ* in Shivalli Tulu and to *r* in Sapaliga Tulu ch 4 (1).
58. Change of *l* to *r* intervocally in Manipuri ch 3 (39).
59. Change of intervocalic *l* to *ḷ* and *ll* to *l* in Marathi ch 3 (13).
60. Metathesis in Telugu ch 3 (33).

# BIBLIOGRAPHY


Ahlqvist, A. (ed.)

1982. *Papers from the 5th International Conference of Historical Linguistics.* Amsterdam: John Benjamins.

Allen, W.S.

1953. *Phonetics in Ancient India.* London: Oxford University Press.

Andersen, H.

1973. Abductive and deductive change. *Language* 49, 765–93.

Anderson, J.M.

1973. *Structural aspects of language change*, Ch. 3, 4. London: Longmans.

——— 1974. *Historical Linguistics II: Theory and description in phonology*. Amsterdam: North-Holland.

Anderson, J.M. and Jones, C. (eds.)

1974. *Historical linguistics I: Syntax, morphology and comparative reconstruction.* Amsterdam: North-Holland.

Anttila, R.

1972. *An introduction to historical and comparative linguistics.* New York: Macmillan.

——— 1977. *Analogy*. The Hague: Mouton.

Arun, V.B.

1961. *A comparative phonology of Hindi and Panjabi.* Ludhiana: Panjabi Sahitya Akademi.

Baldi, P. (ed.)
1991. *Patterns of change, change of patterns: Linguistic change and reconstruction methodology.* Berlin: Mouton de Gruyter.

Baldi, P. and R.N. Werth (eds.)
1978. *Readings in historical phonology.* University Park: Pennsylvania State University.

Beames, J.
1872–9. *A comparative grammar of the modern Aryan languages.* Reprinted in 1970 by Motilal Banarsidass, Delhi.

Bellugi, U.
1971. Simplification in children's language. In: Huxley and Ingram, (eds.) *Language acquisition: Models and methods*, 95–119. London: Academic Press.

Bellugi, U. and R. Brown (eds.)
1964. *The acquisition of language.*Chicago: University of Chicago Press.

Bever, J.G. and D.T. Langendoen.
1971. A dynamic model of the evolution of language. *Linguistic Inquiry* 2, 433–63.

Bhat, D.N.S.
1968. Is sound change gradual? *Linguistics* 42, 5–18.

_____ 1970a. A new hypothesis on language change. *Indian Linguistics* 31, 1–13.

_____ 1970b. Review of King 1969. *Indian Linguistics* 31, 49–57.

_____ 1971. Hoenigswald's patterns of sound change. *Indian Linguistics* 295–300.

_____ 1972. *Sound change.* Poona: Bhasha Prakashan.

_____ 1974. Retroflexion and retraction. *Journal of Phonetics* 2, 233–7.

_____ 1974b. The phonology of liquid consonants. *Working Papers on Language Universals* 16, 73–104.

_____ 1975a. The basis of comparative method. *Language Sciences* 35, 15–21.

—— 1975b. Two studies on nasalization. In: Ferguson, C.A., L.M. Hyman and J.J. Ohala, (eds.) *Nasálfest: Papers from a symposium on nasals and nasalization*, 24–48. Stanford: Language Universals Project.

—— 1976. Dichotomy in phonological change. *Lingua* 39, 333–351.

—— 1978. A general study of palatalization. In: Greenberg, J.H. (ed.) *Universals of human language*, 47–92. Stanford: Stanford University Press

Bhatia, T.K.
1975. The evolution of tone in Punjabi. *Studies in Linguistic Sciences* 5, 12–24.

Bloomfield, L.
1933. *Language*. New York: Holt.

Bonfante, G.
1945. On reconstruction and linguistic method. *Word* 1, 83–94.

Burrow, T.
1955. *The Sanskrit language*. London: Faber & Faber.

Burrow, T. and Emeneau, M.B.
1960. *A Dravidian etymological dictionary*. London: Oxford University Press.

Bybee, J.L.
1980. Morphophonemic change from inside and outside the paradigm. *Lingua* 50, 45–59.

Bynon, J.
1977. *Historical linguistics*. Cambridge: Cambridge University Press.

Chafe, W.L.
1959. Internal reconstruction in Seneca. *Language* 35, 477–95.

Chatterji, S.K.
1926. *The origin and development of the Bengali language*. Part 1, Ch.2. Reprinted in 1970 by George Allen and Unwin Ltd., London.

Chen, M.Y and W.S.Y. Wang
1975. Sound change: actuation and implementation. *Language* 51, 255–81.

Christie, W.M. Jr. (ed.)
1976. *Current progress in historical linguistics*. Amsterdam: North-Holland.

Croft. W.
1990. *Typology and universals.* Cambridge: Cambridge University Press.

Crowley, J.
1993. *An introduction to historical linguistics.* 2nd ed. Auckland: Oxford University Press.

de Chene, B. and S.R. Anderson
1979. Compensatory lengthening. *Language* 55, 505–35.

Dyen, I.
1964. Lexicostatics in comparative method. *Lingua* 13, 230–9.

Fairbanks, G.H.
1970. Language split. *Glossa* 3, 49–66.

Ferguson, C.A.
1963. Assumptions about nasals: A sample study in phonological universals. In Greenberg (ed.) 30–52. Cambridge, Massachusetts: The MIT Press.

Fisiak, J. (ed.)
1978. *Recent developments in historical phonology*. The Hague: Mouton.

——— 1985. *Papers from the 6th International Conference of Historical Linguistics*. Amsterdam: John Benjamins.

Fox, A.
1995. *Linguistic reconstruction: an introduction to theory and method.* Oxford: Oxford University Press.

Fromkin, V.
1970. The concept of 'naturalness' in phonetic theory. *Glossa 4*.

Ghatage, A.M.
1962. *Historical linguistics and Indo-Aryan languages.* Pune: University of Poona.

Goyvaerts, D.L.
1975. *Present-day historical and comparative linguistics.* Gent: E. Story-Scientia.

Greenberg, J.H. (ed.)
1963. *Universals of language.* Cambridge, Massachusetts: The MIT Press.

——— 1966. Synchronic and diachronic universals in phonology. *Language* 42, 508–17.

——— 1969. Some methods of dynamic comparison in linguistics. In Puhvel, J. (ed.) *Substance and structure of language,* 147–203. Berkeley: University of California Press.

Gudschinsky, S.C.
1951. The ABC's of lexicostatistics (Glottochronology). *Word* 12, 175–210.

Haas, M.R.
1969. *The prehistory of language.* The Hague: Mouton.

Haugen, E.
1950. The analysis of linguistic borrowing. *Language* 26, 210–31.

Hock, H.H.
1974. Historical change and synchronic structure: The case of the Sanskrit root nouns. *International Journal of Dravidian Linguistics* 3, 215–28.

——— 1985. Regular metathesis. *Linguistics* 23, 529–46.

——— 1986. *Principles of historical linguistics.* Berlin: Mouton de Gruyter.

Hockett, C.F.
1950. Age-grading and linguistic continuity. *Language* 26, 449–57.

——— 1958. *A course in modern linguistics.* New York: Macmillan.

——— 1965. Sound change. *Language* 41, 185–204.

Hoenigswald, H.M.

1960. *Language change and linguistic reconstruction*. Chicago: University of Chicago Press.

_____ 1965. Phonetic reconstruction. In: *Proceedings of the Fifth International Congress of Phonetic Sciences*, 25–42. Basel: Karger.

_____ 1973. *Studies in formal historical linguistics*. Dordrecht: D. Reidel.

Hogg, R.M.

1976. The status of rule reordering. *Journal of Linguistics* 12, 103–23.

Hörmann, H.

1970. *Psycholinguistics: An introduction to research and theory*. English translation by H.H. Stern. New York: Springer.

Huxley, R. and E. Ingram (eds.)

1971. *Language acquisition: Models and methods*. London: Academic Press.

Jakobvites, L.A. and M. Miron

1967. *Readings in the psychology of language.* Englewood Cliffs, N. J.: Prentice-Hall.

Jakobson, R

1941. *Child language, aphasia and phonological universals*. English translation by A.R. Keiler, 1968. The Hague: Mouton.

_____ 1962a. The concept of the sound law and the teleological criterion. *Selected writings* 1, 1–2. The Hague: Mouton.

_____ 1962b. Typological studies and their contribution to historical comparative linguistics. *Selected writings* 1, 523–32. The Hague: Mouton.

Jankowsky, K.R.

1972. *The Neogrammarians: A re-evaluation of their place in the development of linguistic science*. The Hague: Mouton.

Jasen, T.

1983. Sound change in perception and production. *Language* 59, 18–34.

Jeffers, R.J. and I. Lehiste
1979. *Principles and methods for historical linguistics.* Cambridge, Massachusetts: The MIT Press.

Jones, C. (ed.)
1993. *Historical linguistics: problems and prospectives.* London: Longman.

Katicic, R.
1970. *A contribution to the general theory of comparative linguistics.* The Hague: Mouton.

Katre, S.M.
1968. *Problems of reconstruction in Indo-Aryan.* Simla: Indian Institute of Advanced Study.

Keiler, A.R. (ed.)
1972. *A reader in historical and comparative linguistics.* New York: Holt, Rinehart and Winston.

Kentowitz, M.
1994. *Phonology in generative grammar.* Oxford: Blackwell.

King, R.D.
1969. *Historical linguistics and generative grammar.* Englewood Cliffs, N.J.: Prentice-Hall.

Kiparsky, P.
1968. Linguistic universals and linguistic change. In. Bach, E. and R.T. Harms (eds.), *Universals in linguistic theory*, 171–202. New York: Holt.

_____ 1970. Historical linguistics. In Lyons, J. (ed.). *New horizon in linguistics*. Harmondsworth: Penguin.

_____ 1978. Analogical change as a problem for linguistic theory. *Studies in Linguistic Sciences* 8, 77–96.

_____ 1988. Phonological change. In: Newmeyer, (ed.) *Linguistics: The Cambridge survey, vol I: Linguistic theory: foundations,* 363–415. Cambridge: Cambridge University Press.

_____ 1995. The phonological basis of sound change. In: Goldsmith, J.A. (ed.) *The handbook of phonological theory.* Oxford: Blackwell.

Krishnamurti, Bh.

1978. Areal and lexical diffusion of sound change. *Language* 54, 1–20.

_____ 1978. On diachronic and synchronic rules in phonology. *Indian Linguistics* 39, 252–76.

Kuryłowicz, J.

1964. On the methods of internal reconstruction. *Proceedings of the Ninth International Congress of Linguists*, 9–36. The Hague: Mouton.

Labov, W.

1963. Social motivation of a sound change. *Word* 19, 273–309.

_____ 1981. Resolving the neogrammarian controversy. *Language* 57, 267–308.

_____ 1994. *Principles of linguistic change: 1. Internal factors.* Oxford: Blackwell.

Lass, R.

1980. *On explaining language change*. Cambridge: Cambridge University Press.

Lehmann, W.P.

1963. *Historical linguistics: an introduction.* Reprinted in India in 1968 by Oxford & IBH Publishing Co., New Delhi.

_____ 1982. *Perspectives in historical linguistics*. Amsterdam: John Benjamins.

Lehmann, W.P. and Malkiel, Y. (eds).

1968. *Directions for historical linguistics*. Austin: University of Texas Press

Macken, M.A.

1995. Phonological acquisition. In: Goldsmith, J.A. (ed.) *The handbook of phonological theory*, 670–96. Oxford: Blackwell.

Malkiel, W.

1962. Weak phonetic change, spontaneous sound shift, lexical contamination. *Lingua* 11, 263–75.

_____ 1968. *Essays on linguistic themes.* Berkeley: University of California Press.

_____ 1976. Multi-conditional sound change and the impact of morphology on phonology. *Language* 52, 757–78.

Marchand, J.W.
1956. Internal reconstruction of phonemic split. *Language* 32, 245–53.

Martinet, A.
1952. Function, structure and sound change. *Word* 8, 1–32.

Masica, C.P.
1991. *The Indo-Aryan languages.* Cambridge: Cambridge University Press.

McMahon, A.M.S.
1994, *Understanding language change.* Cambridge: Cambridge University Press.

Mehendale, M.A.
1960. Limitations of the method of internal reconstruction. *Indian Linguistics* 21, 101–3.

Meillet, A.
1967. *The comparative method in historical linguistics.* English translation by G.B. Ford, Jr. Paris: Champion.

Miranda, R.V.
1975. Internal reconstruction: scope and limits. *Lingua* 36, 289–306.

Murrey, R.W.
1982. Consonant cluster developments in Pāli. *Folia Linguistica Historica* 3, 163–84.

Osgood, C.E. and T.A. Sebeok (eds.)
1965. *Psycholinguistics: A survey of theory and research problems.* Bloomington: Indiana University Press.

Palmer, L.R.
1972. *Descriptive and comparative linguistics: A critical introduction.* London: Faber & Faber.

Penzl, H.
1957. The evidence for phonemic changes. In: E. Pulgram

(ed.) *Studies presented to Joshua Whatmough*, 193–208. The Hague: Mouton.

Postal, P.M.
1968. *Aspects of phonological theory*. New York: Harper and Row.

Puhvel, J. (ed.)
1960. *Substance and structure of language*. Berkeley: University of California Press.

Pulgram, E.
1959. Proto-Indo-European reality and reconstruction. *Language* 35, 421–6.

_____ 1961. The nature and use of proto-languages. *Lingua* 10, 18–32.

Rauch, I. and G.F. Carr (eds.)
1983. *Language change*. Bloomington: Indiana University Press.

Rutherford, W.E.
1984. *Language universals and second language acquisition*. Amsterdam: John Benjamins.

Sapir, E.
1921. *Language: an introduction to the study of speech*. New York: Harcourt.

Sebeok, T.S. (ed.)
1973. *Current trends in linguistics*, Vol. 11: *Diachronic, areal and typological linguistics*. The Hague: Mouton.

Smith, F. and G.A. Miller (eds.)
1966. *The genesis of language: psycholinguistic approach*. Cambridge, Massachusetts: The MIT Press.

Smith, N.V.
1981. Consistency, markedness and language change: on the notion of "consistent language". *Journal of Linguistics* 17, 39–54.

Stockwell, R.P. and Macaulay, R.K.S. (eds.)
1972. *Linguistic change and generative theory*. Bloomington: Indiana University press.

Sturtevant, E.H.

1917. *Linguistic change: an introduction to the historical study of language.* Chicago: University of Chicago Press.

Traugott, E.T., Labrum, R. and Shepherd, S. (eds.)

1980. *Papers from the 4th International Conference on Historical Linguistics.* Amsterdam: John Benjamins.

Turner, R.L.

1966. *A comparative dictionary of the Indo-Aryan languages.* London: Oxford University Press.

Ultan, R.

1971. A typological view of metathesis. *Working Papers on Language Universals* 7, 1–44.

Upadhyaya, U.P.

1976. *A comparative study of Kannada dialects.* Mysore: University of Mysore.

van Coetsem, F. and L.R. Waugh (eds.)

1980. *Contributions to historical linguistics.* Leiden: E.J. Brill.

Wanh, W.S-y.

1969. Competing changes as a cause of residue. *Language* 45, 9–25. (ed.)

_____ 1977. *The lexicon in phonological change.* The Hague: Mouton.

Weinreich, U., W. Labov and M. Herzog

1968. Empirical foundations for a theory of language change. In: Lehmann and Malkiel (eds.), *Directions for historical linguistics* 95–195. Austin: University of Texas Press.

Wrenn, C.

1943. The value of spelling as evidence. *Transactions of Philological Society.*

Wolner, A.C.

1928. *Introduction to Prakrit.* Reprinted in 1975 by Motilal Banarsidass, Delhi.

# INDEX